(R

An Introduction To The Faith Of Catholics

Richard Chilson

PAULIST PRESS
New York/Ramsey

ACKNOWLEDGEMENT

Excerpts from the English translations of the Order of Mass, Rite of Baptism for Children, Rite of Marriage, Rites of Funerals, and Rites for Holy Week, copyright 1969, 1970, International Committee on English in the Liturgy, Inc. All rights reserved.

NHIL OBSTAT
Rev. Charles W. Gusmer
Censor Librorum

IMPRIMATUR
Most Rev. Peter L. Gerety, D.D.
Archbishop of Newark
August 6, 1975

Cover design: Dan Pezza

Copyright © 1972, 1975 by
The Missionary Society
of St. Paul the Apostle
in the State of New York

Library of Congress
Catalog Card Number: 72-81229
ISBN: 0-8091-1873-4

Published by Paulist Press, 545 Island Road, Ramsey, N.J. 07446

Printed and bound in the
United States of America

THE FAITH OF CATHOLICS

Contents

To Ken and Mose—
Christ-bearers to me—
Thanks

Foreword to the Revised Edition

Revised editions are often only perfunctory affairs, particularly if the book in question has been successful. Certainly this book has seemed to meet a need, and its first edition was quite popular. Thus when the editors of Paulist Press first suggested that I revise it, I thought of making only a few corrections of phrase and perhaps adding one or two pages in order to deepen the treatment of certain matters.

But as I began the work of revision I noticed certain inadequacies, at least as regards part of the audience for which the book was intended. Obviously some readers were non-Catholics who wanted to learn more about the Catholic faith. For these people the book seemed quite adequate, needing only a few changes and additions. But there was another audience as well: Catholics who wished to re-examine their faith in the light of the Second Vatican Council. The book was not sufficient for their needs.

The first edition presented a vision of the Catholic experience as reformed by the Second Vatican Council. However, it never dealt with the problems Catholics would have coming to grips with this new vision in the light of their childhood faith. For example, how does our new understanding of Mary compare with her former place in Catholic life and piety?

Naturally in teaching an inquiry course using my book I could add all this information for the benefit of those Catholics present. But how could this book

really help the Catholic who reads it on his own? The
book was not very helpful in such a situation. So in
considering a revision I decided that perhaps we
needed two editions: one for non-Catholics would be
basically the same as the first edition, while the
Catholic edition would contain considerable material
describing the new Church in relation to the old and
our understanding of the faith in the light of Vatican
II as compared to the Baltimore Catechism.

I actually completed both editions and submitted
them to the publisher. However, while the editors
liked the idea, they decided that for reasons of mar-
keting it was unfeasible; there would be confusion
among prospective buyers, confusion in the shipping
department, confusion all around.

Instead they suggested that I combine both books
into one while retaining the specifically transitional
material for Catholics either in an appendix or isolated by italics. The more I think of this idea, the
more it seems not a compromise but the ideal solution. I was afraid to burden the non-Catholic with all
this material from the Catholic past. But this material, this old understanding of the faith, is very much
present in the Church today. Indeed is any description of the faith of Catholics adequate which ignores
the way most American Catholics still view their
faith?

We live in a changing Church. We live in a
Church on the march. We Catholics have the future
form of our faith defined through the Vatican Council documents. But at least today that description is
for the future while most of us continue to wrestle
with the Catholicism we have inherited from our
past. Any person seeking a description of Catholicism today must take into account the changes and

convulsions occurring as this new understanding of the faith comes to maturity.

A changing Church is a confusing Church. This edition of *The Faith of Catholics* does not possess the dignity, the order, the clarity or the compactness of the first edition. And it now differs significantly from every other description of the Catholic faith on the market, for it no longer describes the faith from an ideal standpoint. Rather, it views the Catholic experience from the point of view of living American Catholics. It not only seeks to describe the faith we hope for in our future, but it also hopefully provides a way there from the faith we are living right now.

This book is a journey toward the city of Jerusalem. The descriptions of that city—the vision of a reformed Catholicism—are presented throughout the book in roman type. The descriptions of the actual journey of American Catholics today toward that city are presented in italic type.

Non-Catholics may wish to skip over the italic parts. One can read the book in this way. In so doing, however, you will miss the struggle going on now within most Catholic communities and within most Catholics. You will miss much of what it is like to be a Catholic today. We are a pilgrim people on our way to a city. We invite you: come with us to that land where we're bound. We are a Church in change, a Church confused, but we are above all, in a way we haven't been since the Reformation, a Church filled with life and the Spirit of God.

Introduction 1:

Restless Man, Troubled People

The flow of a man's life

Most of the time we live from day to day: not lives of quiet desperation perhaps, but at least lives that carry us onward in their drift like some huge river. And we float along with the current, seldom thinking about anything: where we are headed, why the river flows, what kind of flotsam or jetsam we might be. We pass much of our life this way and with good reason. For if we did not, we might never make any progress downstream.

Inevitably, however, it happens that bends or rapids crop up in the river. The current shifts, becomes unpredictable, and we are jarred, knocked about, sent shooting forward or caught in a whirlpool that threatens to drag us under. Shaken out of our complacency, we wonder. We cry out, we try to gain our feet, to stand up out of the river. And we ask questions whose answers may have seemed unimportant before. A nine-year-old girl dies of leukemia. A husband is slaughtered in an automobile accident. I fall in love with the most beautiful girl in the world. A young man wakes one morning to realize suddenly that he is a father, that one very weak baby has been given into his rough hands and is totally dependent upon him. At such a moment the awesome question arises. What question? Any vital question, any question about life: Why are we here? Does life have any meaning? What is important in my life? Is death meaningful or is it merely senseless?

The vital question may occur during a great crisis, but often it arises for no reason at all. In either case it shakes us to our very depths. And it is no question easily answered: no simple answer of a few easy words will ease the yearning that has stirred. For we ask not in order to learn some bit of knowledge, but because the answer holds important consequences for our entire life: how we shall look at the world, the way we feel, what we consider good or bad, where we are going.

A sense of loss

Today we American Catholics also find ourselves in a quandary—a crisis. While in other people the vital question of meaning arises out of various life situations, for American Catholics today the question of meaning is often prompted by the enormous changes that have occurred within our religion. Within the last fifteen years changes have taken place which make our religion seem quite different from what it was. And these changes have caused a shift in our attitude toward our faith so that we no longer look on it with quite the same awe or even respect we once had. For Catholics it is our faith itself which has lost meaning and therefore raised the vital question in our lives.

Fifteen years ago we Catholics had little choice. There were three roads open to the American Catholic. I could abandon my faith and my Church and inevitably suffer from tons of guilt. I could be a marginal (and that meant bad) Catholic. In this case I would not live up to all that was expected of me. Yet I would not abandon the faith altogether. I might not go to Mass, but I would consider myself a Catholic. This course always entailed extreme guilt. Or I could be a good Catholic. I would practice my faith —assent to its dogmas, observe its rules, attend its worship—and in return I was assured that my perseverance would find its reward in heaven.

For my religion I was willing to sacrifice. For my religion I had no choice but to sacrifice. For ours was a religion of offering up. We offered up almost anything and everything—from meat on Fridays to the pill that planned parenthood. Now less than fifteen years later "offering up" will earn one not the title of "saint" but the put-down of "neurotic."

All our lives we were told that the liturgy re-enacted the holiest and most sacred moments of our faith. We placed our priests on pedestals; they were men set apart, and their highest calling was to offer the Mass for us. The Latin language was a sacred language—and even then the words were too holy to be mouthed aloud.

Now we are told that liturgy is something we must do along with the priest. We must participate even though our words and gestures might feel irreverent or embarrassing. And even if the new liturgy seems liberating to us, there is still something missing. For most of us the liturgy today is more comprehensible, but the experience and awe of the holy is gone. The magic has gone out of the Mass, and all of us—conservative, avant-garde, or just plain old Sunday pew-sitter—miss it. Mass simply does not have the same place in our lives it had before.

The great laws of fasting and abstinence were changed within a week. One Friday we couldn't eat meat; the next Friday we could. If they can do that with meat on Friday, what's to stop a person doing it with Mass on Sunday? Why should I attend Mass every Sunday? Lightning won't come down from above! And if God is cheap enough to send me to hell over Sunday Mass, then he doesn't deserve to be my God anymore. It's quite simple—I no longer feel obligated.

And suddenly parochial schools are not the answer. In spite of our efforts and sacrifices to keep them open, they are being closed. For years we were told that the only way to ensure our children a good education in the faith involved sending them to parochial schools. Now suddenly this great insurance against apostasy is unavailable.

Thus we are forced to settle for what we always called adequate but only second best: part-time religious instruction. However, the faith they are supposedly learning there does not seem to be the faith we grew up with. We wonder whether our ten-year-old knows the ten commandments. We doubt if he knows the Hail Mary. Does he even know what a rosary is? He does not seem to know his religion at all! Half of the things we were required to memorize in the Baltimore Catechism are totally unknown to him. The great structure of our faith has been watered down to love and charming little stories.

Everything seems to have turned somersaults over

the last few years. It's getting so that we don't know what is "up for grabs" and what is "for keeps" in the faith. Sometimes we think that the only thing that hasn't changed in the new Church is that we are still told from on high what will change and what will not. They told us to keep quiet at Mass; now they tell us to sing and talk and even dance. They told us not to eat meat on Friday; now they tell us to eat meat on Friday. The trouble is that now we wonder whether "they" know any more about what is going on than we do.

A snake in the Mass

A familiar story fits well our current predicament. As Catholics we have traditionally regarded the story of Adam and Eve as completely and historically true; it really happened and in just that way.

However, if we read the story of Adam and Eve as an account of what really happened, of how God created man, or how we arrived in the situation the world is in today, then much of its importance will be hidden from us. Let us consider Adam and Eve not so much a story about what happened once upon a time, but rather in terms of what has happened and is happening to us. Is not the story of Adam and Eve very similar to our story?

In the beginning Adam and Eve are placed in a garden called Eden. This paradise is completely shut off from the rest of the world; it is totally self-sufficient. When we live in paradise we have no concern or curiosity about what is next door. For what could possibly be as good as, not to say better than, Eden?

There were few restrictions placed upon Adam and Eve in Eden. They were simply forbidden to eat of the tree of the knowledge of good and evil. In other words: "Don't get curious; don't rock the boat." That was the only restriction, and it was not too great a price to pay for paradise.

We heard similar words in our youth: "Don't taste of secular knowledge! Don't savor too deeply of the world! After all, look at all those so-called intellectuals who have lost their faith. What has the world got to compare with the truths of the faith shared by no one in the outside world?" With slight exaggeration (and what good story does not indulge in exaggeration to make its point sharper?) this was the attitude of the ghetto Catholicism in which we Americans were raised.

The faith was our Eden and worth a few paltry sacrifices. But whether we were obedient to the laws of this Catholic paradise or not seems not to matter. There was a snake in the grass of our garden, just as there was in the garden of Eden, and our forbidden fruit was eaten too—by intellectuals, by theologians, by priests, and even by bishops. These people wished to gaze outside paradise and see what was there. And it seems that because of their transgression we have all forfeited the garden and must count paradise as lost.

We Catholics are now part of that once forbidden world. Our ghetto of Eden is gone. No longer do there seem to be any prohibitions. The laws we once thought divine now are seen to be all too human. Today even the law on divorce and remarriage is being challenged. Some have tasted of the tree of the knowledge of good and evil, and now we must all go around in fig leaves.

No longer are we a separated people. We are just like the rest of men. In the past we were often regarded with either awe, scorn or incomprehension. Today we form simply another statistic. We hardly vary significantly from the national norm, whether the survey be on Sunday worship attendance, divorce and remarriage, or even belief in God!

We used to be a law-abiding people. The laws and dogmas of Catholicism gave security because they were universal and unchanging. Then all of a sudden there were law-breakers in our midst—and they were priests and nuns. They first broke the civil laws, but soon not even Church laws were exempt. From burning draft board files in defiance of the state, they turned to marriage in defiance of the Church. Granted the laws were sometimes difficult to follow, but the reward was salvation. We never considered ourselves in prison. However, now someone has flung open the door and shouted: "We have freed you!" Can you blame us if we feel lost?

The persistence of life's question

The question lurks in each of us. It rises to the surface of our life in many different ways. Some spend their whole lives seeking an answer to satisfy the great question that drives them. Others only become aware of the question at a certain point of their life, at certain peak or crisis moments. And for them perhaps the question is easily answered. They find peace in the religion in which they were reared; they discover an answer in a life of social service or in the love of another person and the security of a family. Still other men suppress the question: should it ever arise in their lives they ignore it, brush it aside, or run until it is left far behind. But although the routine of daily living or the hedonism of drugs and alcohol may submerge the yearning, it still lurks in us, demanding an answer.

No ordinary question this. It is not just a question of the head or a matter of the stomach that can be satisfied through a simple word or a crust of bread. Our whole being is brought into question. If my child has been killed in a freak accident I want to know why; no pat intellectual answer about the inscrutable workings of the universe will satisfy my anger and rage against such a senseless tragedy.

Our yearning is not just a question of knowledge nor is it a longing of our senses. In the presence of beauty and joy we may, overwhelmed, momentarily forget the yearning within us but soon we will wonder again. What of this very beauty? Why is it here? Why does it speak to me so deeply? Yet what is its message that I only half hear?

Another person may quell this yearning and so I hope as I fall in love and lose my self and my question in the beloved. But soon again it rises to the surface. Human love is fragile. Often it breaks under the simple strains of daily living. Or in the middle of the night I awake to a vision of its fleetingness. For this love of mine, my shelter from life's cruelty and unconcern, is only human too. She shares the same fears, the same yearnings. Can we love and play in the sand only to die and have our frail castles washed away, our fleeting moments forgotten forever?

But perhaps I can build for the future. There are my children; they will be my hope and my faith. In them I shall not die; I shall not have lived in vain. And so I am triumphant until one day in their eyes I perceive that dread yearning I have known so well. And what shall I tell them, what shall I give to them that will not disappoint or disillusion?

This yearning and this restlessness, this insistent question appears to be the only certainty we have about ourselves. I am a man: I question. After that silence? Perhaps we should take the question as the center of our life. Is this man's greatness, that he can never be satisfied, that he is ever driven on to new heights, new peaks of experience? He is an animal with a fatal disease, the dis-ease of his eternal question, and this is his genius.

A noble stand! Heroic man against a cold world! But if we live only for the question will we not in the end despair? Such a purpose is insufficient. If life be not more than a gritting of teeth to bear up under the strain, it would well be ended sooner than later. If there is no answer ultimately, then our search now is meaningless. We are condemned to frustration.

A time for questioning

We are still Catholics—albeit confused, dissatisfied ones. Just once we would like to ask a question and receive a straightforward answer: What must we believe today? In other words, what has not changed to which we must still assent? If that question could be answered, we would find our way back to Eden and security.

But will an answer to that question truly help us? It seems like the right question to ask, but is it?

What must *we believe? Is that what we really need to know? We certainly know and hold for certain that we need not believe and hold unchangeable all that we held before. To ask "What must we believe?" means that we want to know exactly what is not changing.*

Let us return to our story of Adam and Eve. They are now, like us, exiled from Eden, and they want to know how to get back in. But if they look around them, they will find out that they are not locked outside the gates of Eden. Rather there are no longer any gates; they can enter the garden of Eden anytime they want. But Eden is no longer the same because it is not protected from the outside world. There are now weeds and insects in Eden just as there are everywhere else.

To return to Eden, Adam and Eve would have to rebuild its defenses and walls. They would have to rid themselves of the knowledge of good and evil. It is doubtful that they would pay so great a price for their former security.

And what about us Catholics? If we are to regain our Eden, we must also rebuild the defenses and walls. Our defense was our dogma, our Catholic faith—unassailable, subduing even reason. And our walls were all the laws that protected our garden from the outside world.

The old bulwark of dogma built safe defenses for faith. It staved off guilt, sin, and insecurity as well as thought, novelty and creativity. Any attempt to reconstruct this bulwark is doomed from the start. The faith we hold today cannot isolate us from the outside world. Never again can we go back to Eden.

And if we would be honest with ourselves, we do

not even want to go back to the garden. We have tasted the wine of freedom, and it is a good vintage. To return to the old Church would mean separating ourselves from our culture. It would involve returning to naiveté, however one manages that! Can we honestly say we would like to be naive again? Could Adam and Eve say they would like to give up their newfound knowledge? Never again can we raise the ramparts and be totally righteous about our faith. To do so we would have to perform a lobotomy upon our last twenty years.

Forward to the city Jerusalem

St. Augustine once said that Adam and Eve were better off for leaving Eden, for only by leaving behind the garden were Adam and Eve and their descendants made ready for the coming of Christ. Reading Adam and Eve in terms of ourselves, could we not say that we American Catholics at this point in our history truly had to leave Eden in order to find Jesus Christ? Could it be that we had to join the twentieth century in order to be saved?

When Adam and Eve left Eden, they embarked upon a journey, but they knew not where. Later prophets in Israel caught a glimpse of the goal, and they discovered that the goal was not a garden but a city. Now it is a lot easier to think of a garden as holy than to consider a city holy. After all, gardens do not have crime, corruption, garbage, and tenements. And yet the vision of the end of our journey in the Old Testament prophets and in the Revelation

*of St. John which concludes our Bible is not of a
garden but of the city Jerusalem.*

*For it is here in our shattered, confusing, dissatis-
fying world and Church that we shall finally be compelled to desire and seek a deliverer and Savior. Out
of the corruption and politics of the city will arise
the kingdom of God. Like Jesus we need the peace
and tranquility of the garden at times in order to
collect ourselves and pray. But the real work is accomplished in the city on a cross, not in the garden
tending the trees.*

A question of meaning

*Our task is not to rebuild the defenses of Eden,
but to go out into the world with Adam and Eve. On
that long journey toward the city, in our insecurity,
in our confusion, in our blindness, we will be compelled to seek the Savior. And our question will not
be: "What must I believe?" That would presume
that we have found the answer and merely want to
defend it. Our question for the journey will rather
be: "What does it mean?" What does the faith I
inherited in the garden mean in my situation today
as I journey toward the city?*

*In the past I knew what my faith meant. It meant
that I was assured of salvation—that I was a part of
my culture and my faith and my family. And yet
today I do not know what salvation means. My faith
often seems irrelevant to my life as an American, as
a worker, even as a member of my family. I really*

feel dissatisfied and insecure because what I do in the Church no longer fits snugly into my overall life. My faith has lost meaning.

Introduction 2:

The Question, The Quest,

The Journey

The religious journey

Our question sets us off on a quest—a religious quest—for religion, despite what we have been told, is simply that dimension of our lives where the question of meaning is posed. Religion interprets for us our question and supplies us with an experiential response, and it is an experiential response we seek. Our problem is not intellectual; if it were, we would not feel uncomfortable sitting in the pew. Our yearning is not a matter only of the mind but of the heart and nerves as well, and religion's response ministers to us as complex human beings.

Let us not mistake what we are seeking. In common language a question seeks an answer, but we do not seek an answer. An answer is wrapped up, sealed and delivered: "Well, the answer to your problem is. . . ." Is that what we really want (even though on the surface that's what we think we want)?

Will a simple answer which demands either assent or denial truly satisfy me? My question, after all, is at root "me." Can it be resolved by anything which is not as whole, as multi-faceted, as mysterious and as personal as "me"? We await not an answer but a response, not a formula or a philosophy but an invitation to life, a religion.

But where shall we discover this religious response? Few indeed are those who have come upon it for themselves. Those few are the religiously gifted who have experienced direct insight into the problem. However, the rest of us lack this intuition, and if we had to await our own insight, we would probably never chance upon our response. Fortunately the wait is unnecessary; responses to our yearning are easily available. Our religiously gifted brothers and sisters have communicated their insights, and from these we may all fulfill our quest.

The end of our quest will lie in an experience of the world: an experience of fear or despair, of awe or love. And when we ask the religious man to share with us his response, he will point toward his experience by means of a story. And in his story will lie an invitation to view the world with the eyes of the story. The story will speak to us on many levels; it will involve us as a total person, and if it seems to proffer a satisfaction for our longing we will enter into the world of the story and we will adopt that religious outlook.

A map of Eden

As we start our journey toward religion we have some initial apprehension. After all religion is a very broad phenomenon and includes many different facets. There are dogmas, rituals, sacraments, scriptures, devotions, prayers, holy days, buildings, or-

ganizations, theologies, music, art, mysticism, and missions, to name just a few aspects of our goal. We could well use a map showing us how to find the goal of our journey—the new Jerusalem. But perhaps we would do well first to look at a map of the garden of Eden where we started out: the old Catholic Church. If we understand better what Eden was like, we can gain some idea how it differs from Jerusalem and also how it is similar. Once we discover that Eden and Jerusalem are very much the same, we will not be so apprehensive about our journey, for we already know a good deal about the new Church simply because we grew up in the old one.

As we have already said, religion begins with a serious question about the meaning of life. Our childhood catechisms knew the importance of questions; they simply made a mistake in both the number and the kinds of questions they asked and answered.

We learned our faith through our educational facilities. Catholic schools were built in order to pass on the faith, and the faith was passed on as though it were simply another course in the curriculum. The faith was a response to hundreds of questions about God, Jesus and life.

These answers were considered dogma—that is, statements about the faith. Strong dogma guaranteed strong faith. One of the distinguishing marks of Catholicism was its system of dogmas. We were a people who sought for clarity in our faith. And we often seemed to be a people who wished to know more and more about God. Some Catholics even hungered for new dogmas in which to believe.

Also in school we learned ethics or Catholic morality. We learned those rules which divided human behavior from Christian behavior—the teachings of the Old Testament and Jesus. And we further learned those rules which distinguished Christian behavior from Catholic behavior—the precepts of the Church. The complex messiness of human action was codified into a clear set of rules. Obedience often seemed to be the one cardinal virtue. And the rules seemed more concerned with "don't"s than with "do"s. Our ethics did a lot to make us Catholic. We were the people who ate fish on Friday, went to Mass on Sunday, abstained from birth control, and didn't believe in divorce. We were the people who were proud to follow the Pope, Christ's vicar on earth.

Our educational resources were also necessary in order to instruct in the worship of the Church. And in the old Church the liturgy could not be appreciated, much less understood, without considerable education. The Mass was what distinguished us most as Catholics. It was our greatest treasure and enshrined our highest mysteries. Yet even the Mass was a great mystery performed with the smell of incense in a language unknown and to a great extent unheard and unseen.

Finally our schools preserved and passed on the stories that made us Catholic. These included the narratives about Jesus and the early Church as well as those about the saints. Even in the old days these inspired us, but then we were children and stories are a child's delight. Grown-ups could be satisfied with dogma but children needed the sugar coating of story. Often enough, however, the tales which most appealed to us as children were the lives of the saints, filled as they were with the bizarre and wonderful, and they had a great influence upon our behavior. *"I want to be just like Rose of Lima. I want to be pure like St. Joseph."* The stories of the saints built good character.

Surrounding and protecting this vast enterprise of religion, like the walls around Eden, were the social institutions of Catholicism. Above all there was the hierarchy of the Church from the Pope on down to the local curate. Here were our custodians, teachers and leaders. The Church was our defense, our salvation, our security, and its well-being was dependent upon a firm organization and obedience to its authority. The Church could not exist without her structure. Sometimes we even considered it divine down to the last monsignor.

At the middle of all this shimmered the experience of Christianity: the feeling of being saved and loved by God. From the heart of our garden flowed a fountain of grace that nourished our being and gave meaning to our world.

We have left the garden of Eden behind. The solid walls of social institution and dogma have come crumbling down, and within those walls things have changed. We look back on our days in the garden with nostalgia, perhaps with regret, perhaps even with bitterness. But those days are ended. We belong now to the world. And if we would again seek meaning from our faith we shall find it not in the secluded garden but in a city called Jerusalem. The map of the city we seek may appear strange. It contains many of the same areas we were familiar with in the garden, but they have changed both position and importance. At first we feel lost in the city. But let us remember the goal of our journey: in the center of the city of Jerusalem also flows a fountain, and in the shimmering, life-giving waters of that fountain

we shall taste again the vision and experience of
Jesus that gives meaning to our lives. The rest of our
book is a journey through Jerusalem on our way to
that fountain. As we come to know this new city,
hopefully you will find it worth building a home in.

We ache for a response to the yearning and confusion in our hearts. We seek some ultimate reality
that we can count on and that will give meaning and
significance to our life. "Ultimate reality" is simply
a more abstract and intellectual term for what people have everywhere spoken of as God.

However, here we hit upon a stumbling block.
Who is God? We certainly thought we once knew
who he was. We had all kinds of pre-conceived ideas
about him, but most of them seem inadequate to us
now. The ideas we received of God in our childhood
now prevent us from really knowing him.

For some even the idea of God no longer has any
real meaning. God has gone on retreat. He has either
disappeared, or he is back in my childhood with the
little old ladies, the rosary beads and the smells of
candle wax and musty incense.

We are still Catholics, but that now seems to
mean something we do on Sundays. It is a feeling we
get sitting in a pew: an hour of nostalgia a week. But
it does not affect the rest of our lives, and recently
what we experience on Sunday often no longer seems
satisfying in itself.

Conversion for the truth-holders

Our situation as American Catholics calls out
today for conversion. It is a conversion that has been
forced upon us, and at first blush it seems silly for

the people who have always prided themselves on
possessing the truth to be in need of conversion.

However, the Second Vatican Council called for
this conversion and initiated it at the top echelons of
the Church. The crisis that called for this conversion
has only now begun to make itself felt at the grass-
roots level. That we are now in crisis no one doubts,
and conversion is a response to crisis. Our lives are
upset; they have lost their equilibrium. Conversion is
an attempt to restore that equilibrium—to reorder
our lives in order to meet the crisis and resolve it.

Conversion is a response to the question raised by
the crisis, an attempt to rediscover meaning after the
upheaval. The crisis question voices our discontent
and our feeling of being lost. It becomes a question
about life and its meaning. It is a vital question as
well as a religious question. We have been forced to
pose it by all the challenging and disconcerting
changes we have experienced recently.

We are in crisis whether we like it or not, whether
we chose to be or not. We can not ignore the crisis,
and we must find some way to make our peace with
it.

We have alternatives, of course. One is that we
could leave the Church. After all, it seems pretty irrelevant. Perhaps it is something we should outgrow.
Or we can for perhaps the first time ask the meaning
of our inherited faith. In childhood we accepted our
religion as something given to us. At that time we
were never given a choice. But today we are put in a
position of choosing whether we want to or not. And
so we pose the question: What does it all mean? And
we seek a response that will once again make faith
worth living.

> *The story of Job in the Old Testament*
> *of the Bible speaks vividly and dramatic-*
> *ally of the vital question. Read the first*
> *three chapters. Our own question may not*
> *be as agonizing or as traumatic as that of*
> *Job, but it is the same question neverthe-*
> *less.*

The Church Praying

Lord,
pour out on us the spirit
of understanding, truth, and peace.
Help us to strive with all our hearts
to know what is pleasing to you,
and when we know your will,
make us determined to do it.
      (Opening prayer—Mass for pastoral or spiritual
meetings)

The Christian Prays

Your pleasure, merciful God—
grant that I may
   desire it ardently,
   learn it carefully,
   recognize it truly,
   fulfill it perfectly,
to the praise and glory of your name.
Lord my God,
give me
   an understanding that knows you,
   a diligence that seeks you,

a wisdom that finds you,
a way of life that pleases you,
a steadfastness that waits for you,
and a confidence that shall at last embrace you.
(St. Thomas Aquinas)

The Christward vision

Our religious quest is for an ultimate reality that we can stand upon and that will give meaning and significance to our life. "Ultimate reality" is simply a more abstract and intellectual term for what people have everywhere spoken of as God. Man's search for God has not changed so drastically during his time on earth. Perhaps we have become more intelligent and refined in our search, but the search itself is everywhere the same.

Whether we are Catholic, Protestant, Jewish or of no religious persuasion, we all have various ideas and concepts of God that we carry around with us. Let us try here at the beginning of our journey to empty ourselves of all our ideas of God—long, gray beards, three persons in one substance, Jesus the judge, keeper of the heavenly books, heavenly clockmaker, whatever. Let us use the word *God* as a cypher, a code word that stands for ultimate meaning. Whatever gives final meaning to my life: that is my God. If we look at our lives today to find our God (and we all have one unless we live totally without meaning or purpose) we shall probably find a different God than the one we might officially believe in. He may be shallow, petty, powerless, poisonous, but if that is where our life's meaning dwells —be it success, money, security, health, or family— there is our God.

Christians seek to follow a God beyond all these
finite sources of meaning, for the gods of money and
success will one day crumble and leave us in chaos.
Only one God is powerful enough to supply our entire existence with meaning, and he too is basically
ultimate meaning—but meaning that will never be
found insufficient or false.

Christians believe that the principle of ultimate reality is a person rather than a thing or an abstract
concept. And they believe that if man has searched
for God in his religions, then, in Jesus of Nazareth,
God on his part has come in search of man. In
Jesus, God has provided us with the true and adequate response to our quest. When the response of
God in Jesus Christ encounters the quest of man for
God, Christianity is born.

Our human question which drives us to seek
meaning in our lives, our question as Catholics
which drives us to re-examine our childhood faith,
draws us to enter upon a pilgrimage in search of
meaning. For Christians and Jews that pilgrimage
has always been described as a journey toward the
holy city of Jerusalem, for in that city God dwells.
Our guide toward the city will be a man named
Jesus. Let us look for a while at life through his eyes.
It is an exciting experience.

Whether you are Christian, Catholic, or uncom-
mitted, for the remainder of this journey do not try
to judge whether the vision is right or wrong. View
the world through Jesus' eyes "as if" what he sees is
so. Suspend your critical distance. Try on the vision
for a while. The only way we can ever truly appreciate a religion is to try it on. This involves no real
commitment on our part. When the journey is done,
if the vision does not prove adequate for you, put it

off and try another vision. But at least by trying on the vision of Jesus you will always have some idea of what it is like to view the world through a Christian's eyes.

Hopefully the vision of Jesus will calm the yearning within us. If we are not yet a follower of Jesus we may find that his vision of life frees us from everything that hems us in. We may find in his message and his love a power that allows us to be reunited with our brothers and sisters as well as the power at the heart of the universe. If we are already Christians, by taking this time to make the voyage of discovery again we will hopefully deepen our appreciation of the vision we share with all other Christians. If we are Catholics, this voyage of rediscovery will reveal to us a new meaning and depth to our religion. We shall find that instead of losing all that was dear to us in the recent changes, we instead have the opportunity as never before to be touched and transformed by a carpenter named Jesus who two thousand years ago left the little village of Nazareth in order to respond to a yearning that cries out in every man, woman and child who ever lived and loved. Jesus gave a name to our yearning and our love: Father. Let us begin our search for our Father in the stories of Jerusalem.

Part I
The Stories of
Christianity

Introduction:

Conversion from Fact to Myth

Out of our disturbance, our confusion, our malaise with current Catholicism, we have been driven toward a question. What meaning can my religion give to my life? In other words, what response can my religion make to me which will give purpose to what I do in the Church as well as to what I do in life?

Such a deep, vital question is best answered not by the dogmatic statements of the old Church but rather by a story. On the surface, stories would seem to be for children. In addition, they are a very ambiguous and circuitous route to a straightforward answer, and such an answer is what we seek.

Yet stories appeal to a much greater part of our human nature than do abstract answers. Dogma addresses only our intellect, and, as we have said, it is not only, or even primarily, our intellects that are troubled by our question.

We Catholics in our recent past have tended to respond to questions not with stories but with dogmas. This was the case with our childhood catechisms. A question such as "What is God like?" was a very good and important question. But the answer we were taught in catechism class—that God is all-powerful, three persons in one essence, and loves us

—certainly did not appeal to our whole being, but only to our mind.

Jesus certainly did not teach like this. He constantly used stories or parables to show people what God was like. He almost never spoke in straightforward language. He was not a philosopher but a poet.

Thus the initial response to our questions will come in the form of stories—both the stories Jesus told and the stories about Jesus himself. In catechism classes for children today the course's content is more likely to be a recital of these stories than a memorizing of dogma. The stories awaken in us an appreciation and love for God that dogma could never do.

And before we listen to a recital of our stories, let us be clear that we are calling them "stories." These are not groupings of facts or journalistic accounts of the way it was, nor are they histories. They are stories, special stories which we might more accurately term "myths."

Unfortunately the word "myth" has become a loaded term in our vocabulary, for we ordinarily think of a myth as a story which isn't true. Now religious stories are seldom true in the sense that they occurred in exactly the same way that the story says they did, but that is a very limited sense of the true.

When we are engaged in myth-telling, we aren't primarily concerned with what really happened. We are concerned about the vital question: What meaning does our life have? Myths give our life shape and meaning. Whether or not they are literally true is beside the point. We listen to myths to find out who we are, why we are alive, where we are going, and *how to get there. Those are the questions religious stories seek to respond to; they aren't concerned with mere facts.*

At first this unconcern for the "facts" may shock us. Our society tends to put a great deal of emphasis upon just those "facts." But in the past we Catholics often seemed more concerned about the facts than the meaning, and we were in danger of missing the forest for the trees. Let us take our question and enter the gates of the new city Jerusalem. Let us become like children again as we ask our question of the old Israelite who sits by the city gate.

1

The Stories
of the Israelites

Christianity's story is of a man and a people, which is built in turn upon the story of a God and a nation. The man is Jesus and his people the Church; the God is Yahweh and his people the nation of Israel. Although we shall be principally concerned with Jesus, we can not ignore Israel, for the Christian experience arose out of Israel and her experience of God. So in answer to the vital question "What is the meaning of life?" a Christian first tells the history of Israel.

The exodus from slavery

To this day every year at the great festival of Passover as each Jewish family gathers to eat the Passover supper, the youngest child in the family asks a question, "Why is this night different from all other nights?" This different special night hides the mystery of Israel's religion, for this night remembers an historical event at the beginning of history which has given purpose and meaning to the life of every Jew.

Some three thousand years ago a leader rose up among a group of slaves in Egypt. This leader, whom tradition names Moses, led a revolt against the Pharaoh, Egypt's ruler. Heading the slaves, Moses inspired them to escape and flee Egypt. He called them to cast off their bondage of slavery. The slaves attributed their success in the escape to Moses' God. They experienced him as a God who had saved them from their taskmasters and had led them into freedom.

The exodus occurred during Israel's heroic age: about the same time as the Trojan war related in the Homeric epics. However when the story is first written down we are far from the age of Moses. The story of Moses, his God and the escape had been passed on carefully from generation to generation because in these events the people saw the birth story of their nation. During centuries of retelling naturally the narrative became more elaborate. Details were added. Dialogue between characters was invented. Certain episodes grew and took on tinges of the supernatural and miraculous.

The slaves had probably escaped, slipping out unnoticed at night. When Pharaoh discovered the ruse he set out in pursuit with his chariots. One of Egypt's boundaries was the Sea of Reeds, a marshy strip of land along the Sinai peninsula. Being on foot, the fugitives could walk through this marsh without becoming stuck, but Pharaoh's horses and chariots became embedded in the mud, and the slaves eluded their pursuers.

In the course of the ages these details were magnified in order better to impress upon the listener how great a victory God had brought about. The Sea of Reeds becomes the Red Sea, a different body of water altogether. Now Moses, standing at the edge of the Red Sea, prays to his God and stretches forth his hands. Miraculously the waters part, permitting the people to walk through the middle of the sea on dry land. When Pharaoh and his army attempt to follow, God causes the waters to rush together again, drowning the entire Egyptian army.

The importance of meaning

Such blatant elaboration shocks us. As modern men our primary concern is with what actually happened. Did these people go through the Red Sea or the Sea of Reeds? Did the waters part for them or not? If the first is the true account, then is not the embellished version not as valid, even false?

But we must remember that the ancient Israelites, retelling their story, were not concerned with the details so much as with the meaning of what had happened. They discovered that this historical event held a meaning for them which gave purpose to their life together. In the exodus they found a power, a God who rescued them and gave them freedom. Previously they had been slaves, now they were free. This freedom experience forms the story's central core; whatever strengthens its impact upon the reader is welcomed.

Looking at the story in terms of its central meaning, there is little difference between the version of what "actually" happened and the more elaborate, embellished account. The latter telling is even preferable since it communicates the message more forcefully and convincingly.

The God of the mountain

In the exodus event the people experienced their God as a savior and a deliverer. But this was only the beginning. The God of Moses now promises to create out of this mass of slaves a new nation. Centuries later the Israelites remembered and relived their nation's birth in the story of the giving of the law to Moses on the top of Mount Sinai.

Escaping the Egyptian army, they had fled into the wilderness and desert of the Arabian peninsula. There, eventually, they pitched camp at the base of the mountain and Moses went up into the mountain. There, amid thunders, lightnings and tremors of the earth, as the later accounts describe it, God made a covenant with the people.

This covenant or constitution set up a nation. A set of laws was concluded between God, the ruler, and his people by which a state was brought into being and governed. The famous code of Hammurabi, formulated about the same time as Israel's Law, is similar to Israel's covenant.

God reminds the people of what he has done for them: he brought them out of Egypt and made them free men. In return they owe him their obedience. Now, for their obedience God promises to form them into a nation: a nation that shall endure as long as the terms of the covenant are not broken.

A new experience of God emerges. The God known to the people as their rescuer and deliverer was now to become their ruler, their king. On Mount Sinai is forged a constitution, a law for their government. God will be their leader and ruler; he will lead them to a land they can occupy as their own. In return he demands to be worshiped as their sole God. Israel and its religion are grounded on this covenant, and throughout their history the Israelites will understand whatever happens to them in the light of this original covenant when God chose them to be his people.

Under Moses's successor, Joshua, the Israelites began to raid and plunder the land of Canaan, located approximately where modern Israel lies. A series of bloody wars ensue which continue for many generations until finally the native people are conquered and victory given to the Israelites. God has been faithful: he has given them the land.

Israel: a nation like all others

Once a landed nation, however, the Israelites soon forgot their original covenant with God. Adopting the local gods of Canaan, they are almost totally absorbed into the native population. Israel demands to have kings like the other nations, and her kings, like other monarchs, are concerned to consolidate their power and to build up wealth. Israel becomes a secular state: her old dependence upon the tribal Yahweh is soon forgotten.

The prophetic experience

During her period of prosperity another experience of God begins to develop. A series of prophets arise in Israel. These men, speaking in the name of God, call the people to return to the Lord and to his covenant. They accuse Israel of having violated the covenant upon which her existence is based.

But things are going well in Israel and the prophets' messages go unheeded. As time goes on, the message becomes more and more harsh. If the Israelites do not change their ways God will abandon them; he will no longer shield Israel but will deliver her up to her enemies.

The prophets experience God as all-powerful and as the controller of history. Slowly the idea develops that this God of Israel is more than simply one tribal God among many. He has control over all nations, not just Israel, but he loves Israel and her he has chosen. But now since Israel has abandoned God, he will in turn desert her.

And Israel soon collapses. Splitting first into two small nations, she is finally conquered by the Babylonians. Her land is burned and most of the people are deported into captivity in Babylonia. The dream of Israel had come to an end; gone is the glory and the power. Once again they are slaves, their freedom something to weep over. The God who once saved them has forsaken his people.

But even in exile the prophets continue to interpret to the people what is happening to them. In their prosperity and glory they had no use for God, so he has delivered them over to the enemy. Now in their captivity they may once more be ready to hear God and return to him.

The prophets saw Israel's defeat as a punishment for her failure to live up to the covenant. Now her captivity and slavery become means for purifying and remolding the people—during this time they once more realize their dependence upon God and they experience the power of God over all nations.

At the same time Israel begins to experience the mercy of God. In spite of everything he loves this people, and he is unable to forsake his nation forever. God does forgive, and after the captivity and the exile he will once again establish Israel as a nation. In her exile Israel learns hope. She learns that the future depends not on her but on God who has control of the future. And finally she begins to realize the great love of God. He can be wrathful and angry but he is also loving and ready to forgive.

Wisdom and hope

In addition to the prophets, Israel had other experiences of God. During her brief glory, Israel began to cherish the cultivation of wisdom. A group of men connected with the royal court devoted their lives to probing the implications of a good and God-fearing life. Proverbs and maxims were collected which guided the people in right living. And the wise men meditated upon the infinite wisdom of God that had brought into being the entire universe and that governs the life of men and nations.

The wisdom literature exhibits a deep knowledge. In it man confronts the questions that arise as he attempts to perceive God's influence upon the world. Why does God allow evil to flourish? Why are good men allowed to suffer? Through meditation upon such difficult problems Israel enriched her faith and came to experience more deeply the rich mystery of life. Her faith in God's guiding wisdom comes to fulfillment in Christianity, in Jesus whom Christians see as the incarnation of God's wisdom.

In Israel's suffering and exile another type of literature is born: apocalyptic. It speaks of crisis and disaster; it foretells the end of the nations in terrifying images of bloodshed, famine and desolation. But apocalyptic is really a literature of hope. For to the oppressed people it promised the collapse of their enemies' power. It offers the hope that God will again rescue his people and lead them out of slavery's darkness into the light.

Israel believed that her hope was fulfilled when the Persian king, Cyrus, restored Israel as a nation. But she never achieved a fraction of her former glory, and after a brief period of independence she is once again conquered, first by the Greeks, then by the Romans.

Her experience of apocalyptic hope in the future grows. Looking back on her past, she sees the image of her greatness in King David who brought her to the height of her power. Now in her weakness and helplessness, she hopes in the promises God made through his prophets: a new leader will come, as great if not greater than David. Under this new leader, whom the Jews refer to as the Messiah, once again God's people will witness greatness. Israel is subjected to Roman dominion but she eagerly awaits the Messiah, a new Moses to lead his people to freedom from slavery, a new David to bring back the glory of past days. During this period of waiting a man Jesus is born.

Israel's faith

Israel forms an insignificant power in world history. She only enjoys her brief period of glory under

David because at that time there were no powerful neighbors around. She has produced little great art or thought compared to Greece or Rome. Her only fame is her experience of God. For Israel read her history, her glories and defeats, in terms of God. And in her history she comes to know this God intimately. He is first a savior, a God who brings man into freedom. Next at Sinai she comes to know and accept him as her king and ruler. As she proves faithless to the covenant, he shows himself as angry and as the controller not only of Israel's destiny but as the Lord of all peoples. When the nation is destroyed and carried off into exile, God becomes the comforter of his people. He becomes Lord of the future when he will once again bring his people from slavery to freedom. Finally, in his prophets, he shows himself as a force of love, fidelity and trust. Israel comes to know that she cannot depend upon herself or other men, but only upon God. Only he is worthy of obedience and loyalty. Only he will not finally disappoint.

Our quick retelling of Israel's story is merely a suggestion of the richness of her experience. Her full witness to that experience is found in the collection of books known to Christians as the Old Testament. There are her stories, her songs, her prophets' writings, the wisdom of her sages. We invite you to let these writings witness for themselves the experience they serve.

The stories of the exodus and of Sinai are presented most dramatically in Exodus 14:5-31 and Exodus 19 and 20.

Jeremiah's prophecies of doom and hope are found in Jeremiah 3:1-18.

Wisdom's song in Proverbs 8:22—9:18 shows the beauty of Israel's meditation on God.

And her future hope is seen in Isaiah 52:1-13.

The Church Praying

Christian worship, like the rest of the Christian religion, rests upon Jewish ritual and liturgy. The following prayers of thanksgiving from the offertory of the Catholic Mass have roots in ancient Jewish prayers from before the time of Jesus.

Blessed are you, Lord, God of all creation.
Through your goodness we have this bread to offer,
which earth has given and human hands have made.
It will become for us the bread of life.

Blessed are you, Lord, God of all creation.
Through your goodness we have this wine to offer,
fruit of the vine and work of human hands.
It will become our spiritual drink.

The Christian Prays ▰▰▰▰▰▰

These famous Jewish prayers the Christian can make his own.

The Shema:

> Hear, O Israel, the Lord is our God,
>> the Lord is one.
> And you shall love the Lord your God
>> with all your heart
>> with all your soul
>> and with all your might.

> (Deuteronomy 6:4-5)

Kaddish (said as a prayer for mourners):

> Magnified and sanctified be his great name in the
>> world
>> which he has created according to his will.
> May he establish his kingdom during your life
>> and during your days
>> and during the life of all the house of Israel,
>> even speedily and at a near time,
>> and let everyone say, Amen.
> Let his name be blessed forever and to all eternity.

> Blessed, praised and glorified,
> exalted, extolled and honored,
> magnified and lauded be the name of the Holy
>> One;
>> blessed be he,
> though he be high above all the blessings and
>> hymns,

praises and consolations,
which are uttered in the world,
and let everyone say, Amen.

He who makes peace in his high places,
    may he make peace for us and for all Israel,
and let everyone say, Amen.

The Blessing of Aaron (known to Christians as the Blessing of St. Francis):

May the Lord bless you and keep you;
the Lord make his face to shine upon you,
    and be gracious unto you;
The Lord lift up his countenance upon you
    and give you peace.

                                    (Numbers 6:24-26)

2

The Stories

of Jesus

The state of Israel has been reduced to a province of the Roman Empire. The Jews maintain an uneasy relation with their conquerors: tension is always present and could flare out into the open at the slightest provocation. The Jewish people live on in the hope of a Messiah, a leader who will drive out the Romans and re-establish the glory of Israel. Many also believe the end of the world is near. They expect any day that events will occur which are sure signs of the end.

"A voice in the wilderness'

Into this situation comes a man named John. He refers to himself as "a voice crying in the wilderness," and he says his work is to "prepare the way of the Lord." He calls on the people to come back to God, to be sorry for their sins, to make amends and change their lives. The last days are here: God has already put the axe to the tree, and soon it will come crashing down.

John is a rough man: his is no message of comfort. He lives in the desert on a diet of locusts and honey; prophet seems to be the only appropriate description of him. Yet there have been no prophets for hundreds of years.

The man has a charisma and fascination about him and he picks up followers. They come and accept his ceremony of baptism. John stands in the middle of a stream and calls out to the people. Those who wish to change their lives, to be dedicated to God, come out to the prophet in the water. He submerges them in the stream as a sign that they wish to be cleansed of their sins and begin a new life.

One day as he is baptizing in the Jordan River a man presents himself to John for baptism. As John is about to perform the action, he suddenly stops, for there is something unusual about this man. Such a feeling of holiness pervades him that it almost seems possible to touch it. John hesitates. "Shouldn't you rather baptize me?" he asks. "Go on with the ceremony," replies the stranger. And John complies. After the rite the man walks out of the river and disappears again into the crowd.

The man and his message

The man is Jesus, a Jew, about thirty years old, from the small village of Nazareth. Soon after his baptism he begins to attract attention as a wandering teacher. He attracts to himself a small coterie of men and women who follow him around the countryside and look to him as their leader and teacher. Jesus and his band of disciples wander from village to village much as numerous other teachers were doing at the same time.

His message was similar to John the Baptist's. He spoke of an approaching kingdom of God, of a new day for Israel. He used much of the popular religious imagery of his day which considered the world near its end. He demanded a change of heart from the people: a change of heart based on the principle of love: love for God and love for one's brother. He spoke of God as a Father, and he wanted all men to come to the realization that they were all children of God and therefore brothers of one another.

In addition Jesus had the power of healing. He was able to restore sight to men who had been blind since birth. A Roman centurion came to him once to ask for his help. His son was sick and could die. Would Jesus please help the boy? Jesus simply tells the centurion that his son will recover, and miraculously the boy, far away at home, recovers at that instant.

A sign of contradiction

Given his message and his healing powers, Jesus should have been extremely popular. After all there is nothing more true, even trite, than to speak of the brotherhood of man and the fatherhood of God. One modern theologian has gone so far as to call the phrase by its initials, BOMFOG. The message is innocuous. Further, a man reported to possess curative powers should never lack for an audience.

But this wandering preacher has certain personality traits and a slant on things that does not sit well with many. John the Baptist has been thrown into prison and beheaded in reward for his work, and Jesus was not so naive as to suspect that he would be received differently.

To speak of the brotherhood of man is fine as long as one remains at the level of generalities. But Jesus quickly moves into specifics, and he often concludes by denouncing the way of life of the Pharisees and the Scribes, two powerful classes in Jewish society. He sides openly with the poor, the beggars, the sick, and other undesirable elements of his society. He does not preach a revolution by violent overthrow of the state, but in a time of tense Jewish nationalism he could easily be interpreted as seditious toward Rome.

In addition to his proclivity for the lower strata of society he has a righteousness and cocksureness about him guaranteed either to make one believe in him and what he says or to make one detest him. No one remains non-committal. He is a forceful and dynamic figure, not afraid to assert something simply on the basis of his own authority. He has no doubts that he is completely right, and he employs little tact in confronting those he feels are wrong and in need of reform. It is little wonder that the Jewish leaders of the day found him an extremely dangerous fellow and soon began to plot his death when they saw his potential popularity and success.

Trial and death

Inevitably he is arrested and tried by both the Jewish leaders on religious grounds and by the

Roman leaders on political grounds. He is convicted and sentenced to death. According to Roman custom he is first scourged with whips and then crucified. He is nailed to a cross between two thieves and left there until dead.

The crowd of people as usual plays fickle. Five days before his arrest they had granted him a hero's welcome into Jerusalem; at the trial itself they clamor for his death. His coterie of men and women followers for the most part desert him. The men flee the scene and only the women are brave enough to stand by him till the end.

We can easily imagine the feelings of these disciples. They had each met Jesus and immediately felt their life changed by him. Eagerly they had abandoned their occupations, their homes, even their families, and to travel with him they were content to live like vagabonds. The future was glorious because this man obviously could transform the world. But as they came to know him better they grew less sure just who he was or what he would accomplish. Some expected he would be more political; perhaps he would organize a band of men to overthrow the government as previous leaders had tried. Others hoped his preaching of love, brotherhood, and a return to God might touch all men's lives as it had touched their own. The one thing they could not foresee was total humiliation and defeat: Jesus himself might have imagined this but his disciples were not so insightful.

Just as success seems assured and the entire populace of Jerusalem is about to rally about Jesus, he is suddenly arrested and condemned with no one to plead his case. Indeed, he himself seems to acquiesce in the decision.

Three years dissipate within one week. Small wonder these men lost their reason and fled the whole scene like frightened children. Not many have made such great sacrifices for a noble cause or altered their entire life style for the sake of such a commitment. When this ideal is suddenly shattered before one's eyes, the whole world blurs, nothing makes sense, reality takes on the quality of nightmare.

One numb day, the Jewish Sabbath, or day of rest, passes. The men are either still in hiding within the city of Jerusalem or they have already fled the city and gone back to Galilee to pick up the pieces.

The dawn of new life

The women, on the morning after the Sabbath, go to visit the grave. Words only go so far to communicate what they experienced there. First the women and after them Peter, the head apostle, and finally the other disciples discover that this man who died two days ago is not dead but alive. How do they know? Because they meet him and as a result of that encounter they *know* that he is not dead but alive.

"He has risen from the dead!" they cry. But this way of speaking only begins to point to the profound reality they experienced. When modern men think of someone rising from the dead, they think of a corpse opening his eyes, rising and walking about. Such a concept does not adequately describe the resurrection.

Jesus is not merely resuscitated: he is resurrected and death lies vanquished at his feet. Resurrection for the Jews meant something that would not happen until the end of the world. Then God would raise men from the dead and the glorious reign of God upon earth would begin. Jesus' resurrection told his disciples that that reign of God had begun.

The resurrection stories preserved by the Church are not journalistically accurate accounts of what happened. They are more concerned to communicate the good news of death's conquest than a scientific description of Jesus' resurrected body. But Christians through the centuries have agreed that these stories capture the experience of that Sunday as well as any human words can. The band of men and women who had had their lives shattered on Friday now were convinced that Jesus' death signaled not the end but the beginning. He had died, and in dying he had conquered death. Now he was alive never to die again.

The meaning of resurrection

The disciples believed that Jesus himself, not merely his ideals or his spirit, lives on. They speak of their experience in terms of seeing him, even touching him. Jesus' appearances are miraculous but they are described in material images: seeing, touching, hearing, eating.

But resurrection is not an end in itself: it is an event which brings meaning into man's life. And it produced an extraordinary change in the life of each disciple. On Friday they had run away in fear and cowardice, their dream of the past three years shattered. On Easter to a man they place their lives in the service of Jesus and his message. This service will cost most of them their lives. They die cruelly and far from their homes, but they die in joy even with the realization that at least one of their hopes (the end of the world and the return of Jesus) has not been fulfilled. The only explanation for this new courage is the meaning they derived from Jesus' conquest of death.

In the end all we have is the testimony and consequent lives of these men and women. We can not prove the resurrection one way or another. It calls each man and woman to accept or reject it. It forms the center of the Christian faith, and throughout two thousand years Christians have chosen to live out their lives in its light. They believe that Jesus' rising from the dead provides people with an interpretation of the world, of themselves, of each other, and of God.

These stories not only invite belief. They also possess power to create belief. They convince us and draw us into their framework. They appeal to us not through the logic of the mind but by the wisdom of the heart. These stories are our greatest inheritance from our ancestors, and they are the greatest legacy we can leave our children. These wonderful stories pass on our faith in its fullness. It is the stories of Christmas that awaken in our hearts the warmth of that season in the coldest time of the year. It is the stories of Easter that resurrect Jesus in our hearts on that sparkling, dewy morning that heralds the coming of spring.

Perhaps in our own lives we do not feel sufficiently at home and familiar with the stories of Israel and Jesus. However, we do hear them every time we partake in the eucharist, we see them visualized in the

*paintings and stained-glass windows of our churches,
and they lurk within the pages of our Bibles waiting
for us to read and reread them to ourselves and our
children.*

The core of Jesus' teaching can be
found in the "Sermon on the Plain" of
Luke's Gospel (Luke 6).

Jesus' controversy with the Pharisees is
seen in Luke 20.

The earliest telling of his arrest and
crucifixion is found in Mark 14-15.

In Matthew 28 is the story of the
women at the tomb on Sunday morning.

A story of the disciples' commissioning
is found in Luke 24:36-53.

 **The Church Praying**

Father,
in the wonder of the incarnation
your eternal Word has brought to the eyes of faith
a new and radiant vision of your glory.
In him we see our God made visible
and so are caught up in love of the God we cannot
    see.

God of love, Father of all,
the darkness that covered the earth
has given way to the bright dawn of your Word
    made flesh.
Make us a people of this light.
Make us faithful to your Word,

that we may bring your life to the waiting world.
Grant this through Christ our Lord.
    (Preface and Opening Prayer—Christmas Day)

The Prayers of Jesus

Luke's gospel emphasizes the many times during the course of his ministry when Jesus prays, but Luke actually quotes very few prayers of Jesus. Jesus' first prayer is one of thanksgiving. Christians consider Jesus' life itself one continuous giving of thanks to God in which we join:

> I thank you, Father, Lord of heaven and earth,
> for hiding these things from the learned and the
>   wise,
> and revealing them to the simple.

The next prayer Luke cites occurs just before Jesus' arrest. Here we see the conflict between the desires of Jesus and the will of his Father:

> Father, if it be your will,
>   take this cup from me.
> Yet not my will but your will be done.

On the cross as he is dying Jesus prays twice. First he asks forgiveness of his enemies:

> Father, forgive them;
>   they do not know what they do.

In the second prayer Jesus surrenders himself to God:

Father, into thy hands I commend my spirit.

If we wish to know what prayer is all about, Luke has shown us through these few brief prayers of Jesus the models and the content for our own life of prayer.

The Christian Prays

From the Eastern Christian Churches comes one of the most popular prayers—the Jesus Prayer. This is a very short prayer which is said over and over again until it becomes as natural as breathing.

Lord Jesus, have mercy upon me, a sinner.

3

From Experience

to Expression

The Gospel writers

When the disciples had encountered their risen Lord, they immediately wanted to tell everyone the great news. When we have had a tremendous experience, when something fantastic has happened to us, when our life has been wondrously transformed, we want desperately to communicate this experience to others. And we relay the experience best through telling our story, what happened to us.

The disciples were no different. They communicated to people their experience of Jesus by relating what Jesus had done. But now as they looked back on Jesus' life and ministry, certain events are seen in a different light. Now looking back, Jesus' life shimmers in the transforming experience of his resurrection. The disciples now realize that this man Jesus is truly God himself, and in his earthly life they now perceive glimpses of his divinity to which they had been blind before.

Although the four Gospels narrate incidents of Jesus' life, they are not biographies in the modern sense, just as the stories of the exodus are not modern history. The disciples are more interested in the meaning of Jesus' life and its impact for human existence than in the bare facts. They are more concerned with the Jesus whom they experience now, living and working in them and in other Christians, than in isolating what happened thirty years ago as he walked the shores of Galilee.

The Gospels are not the biography of a dead man, but of a man still alive in the fullest sense of the word. He is alive in his followers, he acts through them, and through them he continues his ministry, his teaching and his healing. The Gospels are witnesses to the experience of the living Jesus; they view his earthly ministry from the vantage point of the current living experience of Jesus in the Christian community.

When we read the Gospels we are reading of the experience Jesus has on the writer's life *as he writes:* in Jesus' life, teaching, example, death and resurrection the evangelist has discovered the response to his vital question. He has experienced in this man a God who loves men so much that he was willing to become a man and die for their sake. He has found that the way to approach his fellow man is as a brother and in love. He knows that he can call the maker of the universe his Father, and that the world did not simply chance to occur nor is it the product of some force, impersonal or even inimicable to us. He knows that now there is a purpose to human life: we are not flickering flames soon to be extinguished forever. Our enemy, death, the thing we most fear and the reality most inevitable and unavoidable, will not be the end of us. We shall pass beyond death and we shall live.

To keep this treasure

The early Christians were all Jews, and the experience they received from Jesus built upon the experience of God and reality they had already come to know in Israel's stories. Jesus became the ultimate and decisive experience of reality, but he built upon and brought to perfection the older traditions. There is a sharpening of focus and a refinement of the Israelite experience in Jesus as well as the decisive event of his resurrection.

So when the Christians set about collecting the various writings which definitively captured their experience of life, they adopted the stories of the Jewish religion and then selected those stories and writings about Jesus and the Christian experience which most perfectly caught and communicated that experience.

As the years passed, the danger of losing the purity of Jesus' vision arose and a list of writings was drawn up by the communities to serve as a norm of the experience. This guaranteed that as the centuries rolled on these selected writings could be used to reach the true experience of Jesus, and they could also be employed to evaluate the contemporary community's faith in terms of the primitive expression. In other words, the Christian community of the year 1200 could come to the original experience of the disciples through these writings, and at the same time they could judge how authentically their own experience of Jesus compared with the original faith.

The holy book

These writings became known as Scripture or the Bible. Christian Bibles are divided into two sections: the Old Testament contains the writings and stories of Israel, and the New Testament the writings and stories of Jesus. Each Testament consists of a number of separate books written at different times. For example, in the Old Testament there are books detailing the history of Israel, books of poetry, books written by Israel's wise men, and books collecting the sayings and lives of the prophets. The New Testament begins with the four Gospels, then the Acts of the Apostles (a history of the first days of the Church which captures the early Christian experience), various letters written by different disciples and Church leaders to Christian communities, and, finally, a book of apocalyptic that provided hope for the early Christians during their time of persecution.

A living tradition

Catholic Christians believe that the Bible is the authentic source and controller of our experience, yet Christian faith is living and not confined to a book. Jesus appeared to his disciples and his resurrection message was passed to other people in different times and places through these disciples and those who succeeded them. Jesus lives in the community that calls itself by his name and participates in his life and experience. The Bible came into existence out of this living community, and it properly belongs to this community. It cannot be divorced from the center of lived Christian experience. The Bible contains Jesus' experience in its most authentic expression and communication: it is truly the Word of God for Christians. But it has its life only for the community gathered together in Jesus' name: for there among men is God truly found.

Catholic and Protestant misunderstanding over Scripture

Martin Luther in the Reformation liberated the Scriptures from the domain of monks and scholars and gave them back to the people. He translated the Bible into German, the language of the people. Before Luther the official version of the Scriptures had been in Latin which was already a dead language, or at least a language only of the educated. Luther's action was decisive for both the history of Protestantism and our own history as Catholics, for the way in which he carried out his reform, as well as the reasons behind the reform, have come between Catholics and the Bible and between Protestant and Catholic accord over the Scriptures until just a few years ago.

First of all, Luther claimed that in order for the people to understand the Scriptures they must be translated into the people's language. To a point this is true. The Catholic Church recognized the validity of Luther's criticism and produced translations such as the Douay-Rhiems version in English. However, that did not mean that before these translations the people knew nothing of the Scriptures or their stories. The stories were kept alive through the ar-

chitecture of the churches whose walls and windows were covered with pictures, statues and sculpture. The Scriptures were also kept alive through the mystery plays which were very important in town life. In an age when ordinary people could not read, the Bible was played, painted and sung.

Secondly, Luther went back to the Greek and Hebrew originals for his translation. This was also an excellent idea, but unfortunately he disparaged the official version of the Church, the Latin Vulgate which St. Jerome had translated from Hebrew and Greek. Luther said that Jerome had distorted the Scriptures. Now Jerome, being human, had made mistakes, but he had certainly not distorted the Scriptures.

Therefore, in order to protect the last thousand years of Christendom from the charge that they did not know the true Scriptures, the Catholic Church was forced to proclaim that St. Jerome's translation was not only good and valid but the official translation of the Latin Church. Thus for a long while all Catholic translations into modern languages were made not from the original languages but from Jerome's translation. Catholics were thus using a translation of a translation, and the vitality of the original Scriptures suffered.

Furthermore, by going back to the original Hebrew for the Old Testament, Luther created yet another difficulty. When Jerome had translated into Latin he had translated the Old Testament not primarily from the Hebrew but from a Greek translation of the Hebrew which many Jews and Christians considered inspired. This Greek Old Testament was known as the Septuagint. And when the Jews formed *their list of books which were to be considered Scripture, they decided that only those books which survived in Hebrew were to be included. This Jewish canon was formed about 200 A.D. in reaction against the Christian canon which had been forming somewhat earlier.*

The Septuagint translation had taken place at least 200 years earlier and thus included books for which the Hebrew originals had now been lost or which were never written in Hebrew at all. Jerome had questions about the books in the Septuagint that no longer possessed Hebrew originals, but he included them in his translation anyway.

However, when Luther went back to the Hebrew, he took only those books available in the Jewish list. He claimed that the other books were of doubtful validity, and he relegated them to a supplement in his Bible.

This created a further division between Catholics and Protestants, since Catholics had been following Jerome's custom of including these books, although realizing that perhaps they were not as important as the other books of the Old Testament. By rejecting these books, Luther forced the issue, and the Catholic response was to define these books as Scripture. The Protestant response was to consider these books as apocryphal or even non-scriptural.

Today all Christian churches are reaching a common understanding concerning Scripture. We recognize with Jerome that these books are not as fundamental to our faith as the other Old Testament books, but at the same time we recognize their value for the information they provide concerning the period between the last Hebrew writings and the first

Christian writings—an epoch of about 200 years.

The Bible also came to be the symbolic focus of the Protestant Reformation. Protestants were people of the book. Thus they forced Catholicism to define itself against this standard. The Catholic Church responded by emphasizing the liturgy as the central font of Catholic life (which it always had been). Unfortunately, however, this emphasis upon liturgy, along with stilted Catholic translations of the Bible, led to a neglect of the Bible by the Catholic people.

The Second Vatican Council took large strides to rectify many of these problems. There are a number of good translations of the Bible from the original languages which Catholics can read today. Almost all these translations are joint efforts between Catholics and Protestants. With the rediscovery of story and its importance in our lives, the Bible should become a much more familiar book to the Catholic people.

A matter of inspiration

Inspiration is another problem which keeps Catholics from feeling comfortable with the Bible today. We were always taught that, unlike any other book, the Bible was a book inspired by God. Therefore the Bible contained nothing but truth.

Now the Bible is filled with facts that contradict one another, and its stories often conflict with a modern scientific understanding of the way things are. How can we believe that creation took place in seven days? that the first man and woman were Adam and Eve? that they did not descend from apes but were created out of the dust of the ground? And did the sun really stand still for Joshua? Did Jesus truly walk on water? Yet the Bible is inspired and therefore supposedly true. Is there any hope that a Catholic could be a fully twentieth-century man?

Let us look closely at the matter of biblical inspiration. What exactly does it say? First of all, it says that the biblical writers wrote under the inspiration of the Holy Spirit. They wrote these books filled with the Holy Spirit. Their books fully and adequately capture the experience of God found in both Israel and Jesus. This does not mean that they worked "out of their mind" totally dominated by some supernatural force. These men were not merely typewriters for God. They were men of their day bound by the scientific knowledge and the cultural and social climate of their times, although they were not writing primarily about science, culture or history but about an experience of God.

The only thing that the inspiration of the Bible guarantees is that the experience of God described in the Bible is an accurate experience. Inspiration says nothing about the truth of the histories related, the accuracy of the science, or the veracity of the anthropology. The Bible may be, and is, false on all these matters when compared with twentieth-century knowledge, but that is not important. What is important is that the Bible today, just as when it was first penned, gives an adequate and true experience of God and of his love for us. It is this experience, mediated through the stories, the poetry, the histories, the prophecies and the theologies, which we should seek whenever we read the Scriptures. These writings have the ability to make the God of Israel and Jesus present in our lives and powerful for the transforming of our vision today.

The Word of the Lord has always been holy and sacred to Jews and Christians. At the beginning of Israel's history Joshua (Moses' successor) gathered the people together, recited their history and led them in renewing their covenant with the Lord (Joshua 24). That covenant was renewed again and again in the course of Israel's history whenever the law (i.e., the Word of God) was rediscovered after a period of neglect or abandonment. King Josiah undertook a reform of Israel's religion once he discovered the law hidden in the wall of the temple after it had been lost and forgotten for generations (2 Kings 22:1—23:3), and the scribe Ezra read from the law of Moses to the people after they returned to Israel from their Babylonian captivity. This event marked the beginning of Judaism—the religion of God's law (Nehemiah 8).

However, God's Word is not dead and buried in a book. It begins as a living word and it continues to give life. To this life and power the prophets Isaiah (Isaiah 6) and Jeremiah (Jeremiah 1:4-19) attest.

Jesus, at the start of his ministry, entered a synagogue and proclaimed the Word of the Lord to the congregation. Then he announced that today the Word had been fulfilled (Luke 4:14-20). Even in New Testament times new writings about Jesus were circulating in the

Christian communities attesting to the divine Word's continued power in human history (2 Timothy 3:14-17).

 **The Church Praying**

The priest prays the following over the deacon before the deacon proclaims the Gospel to the people:

> The Lord be in your heart and on your lips
>   that you may worthily proclaim his gospel.

The Christian Prays

This prayer is said by many Catholics before they begin reading from the Scriptures:

> O God, who instructed the hearts of the faithful
>   by the light of the Holy Spirit,
> grant us in the same Spirit to be truly wise
>   and ever to rejoice in his consolation.

Part II
The Dogmas of
Christianity

Introduction:

From Defenses to Guideposts

Let us look once again at our map of Eden. In the old Church dogma served an extremely important function. It formed the defenses and battlements of our religion along with our social institutions. Dogmas in a sense formed the true content of our childhood faith in a way that the biblical stories did not. The old question-and-answer catechisms upon which we were nourished thrived upon the precise responses and categories of Catholic dogma. Catholic practice was grounded upon the liturgy, Catholic life upon the ten commandments and the precepts of the Church, and Catholic thought upon the dogmatic pronouncements. Catholicism's genius constructed the most reasonable defense for the most absurd act ever to occur upon the face of the earth: God became man.

Catholic belief then became assent to those most reasonable though absurd dogmas. Belief was like trust, for it was trust in knowledge which could not be proven true. We could show how it was reasonable for God to become man, but that he did in actual fact become man we could only believe. We trusted in the knowledge that Jesus was God.

Therefore, when belief collapsed, doubt was born. Nagging, insidious doubt whispered that it might not

be so. *Scientific doubt said that faith was against nature. Doubt was to be avoided, fled from into the security of mother Church, and prayed away by renewed acts of oblation, more fervent prayers and
novenas.*

*This was a mistaken concept of belief, for belief is
really not some inferior kind of knowing, as it would
be were trust in things unprovable. Belief tries to
find meaning in life. Belief attempts to understand
oneself and the world. Belief struggles to make sense
of brute facts and to make our world a home—a fit
place for human habitation.*

*The collapse of belief is not doubt. Doubt is a vital
part of belief, for it challenges us to plumb ever
deeper for meaning. Belief's cancer is not doubt but
despair. Despair claims that there is no meaning in
life, that we are in the hands of the gods, and they
toss us hither and thither like footballs. Despair
counsels surrender, for the world is hostile and ultimately uninhabitable. Despair says that there is no
meaning, and that we might as well die.*

*If to believe is to seek meaning in life, then the
real treasure of our faith is not the dogma but the
stories. Dogmas give knowledge, but knowledge provides meaning for the mind only, and not necessarily
for the spirit. Stories are so much more human than
dogma; they appeal to us on all the levels of our
being—intellectual and emotional. Stories build for
us a home in our world; they make our world familiar; they touch creation with the humanity of meaning. Stories transform forests into cathedrals, the
whirlwind into the voice of God, and death into a
passover into life.*

Dogma will never again be the central concern it was in our childhood. Dogmas are simply signposts indicating how to interpret the different stories. They mark out the limits of our Christian experience. They keep our experience on target. Our dogmas are only signposts along the journey of the stories. They tell us that we are still on the right path. They are important—very important—for without them we might well become lost. However, the road signs are not the villages, the lakes and the mountains. The road signs only point the way and identify where we are and when we are there.

4

To the Depths
of Meaning

The spread of the good news

After the resurrection, the disciples spread the
good news they had discovered in this man and his
life: the good news of a God who cares for us and
who saves us from death, the good news of a goal for
living found in loving—God's love for us and our
love for God and our fellow man. But as they attempted to communicate their experience they found
they had to struggle with words and their meaning.

They began by telling about their Lord. They told
how he died and how God did not forsake him but
raised him from the dead. But almost immediately
they needed to articulate their experience more fully.
A religious experience affects and transforms our
whole life, our entire way of looking at things. It
cannot be relegated to some little corner and brought
out into the open only when useful or needed.

These disciples are no longer the same as they
were before. A new experience has entered their
lives, and they must now reorder their existence in
the light of Jesus. Consider what happens when a

couple marries. Both persons must reorient their lives and habits. Before, each had only himself to consider, but now they are no longer one: they are two.

First the disciples had to understand what the resurrection meant about Jesus. What impact does this event have on the lives and the deaths of the rest of mankind? Who is this Jesus that God should resurrect him? Does his death have a meaning in the light of his resurrection? Such probes into the meaning of their new experience give birth to Christian theology. A Greek word meaning "talk of God," theology is the attempt to explain in precise language the meaning found in the Christian experience.

A search for precision

The first centuries of the Christian religion are overflowing with different theologies, different ways of understanding the experience of Jesus. Again the most obvious parallel is the experience of love between a man and a woman. They experience their love for one another, but they also wish to talk about it, to describe it. One may be a poet and succeed in capturing the love in a poem. An outsider reading the poem will experience an inkling of their love. But the poem is not intellectually but rather experientially precise: it does not explain; it, too, merely *is*. A poem can capture but it does not explain the experience. It is as mysterious as the original love. So the lover may try to put his experience into more precise words: he talks of his love in terms of philosophy or biology or psychology. And employing the precise terms of these disciplines, he might arrive at a precise definition of his love.

But although he gains in precision when he uses scientific words, he at the same time loses the vividness of the original experience. Love can be examined in terms of philosophy or psychology, but each only captures for examination a fragment of the original experience. A poem might actually awaken in the reader a glimpse of love; a scientific analysis explains the experience in part but it cannot kindle it in another.

The Christian, too, wishes to delve into his experience, to mine its riches and bring it to intellectual awareness so that he may discuss it, deal with it, and enable it to penetrate to all points of his existence. Because he is a man, gifted with intellect, he desires to articulate his experience. He wishes to bring it to mind so that he may evaluate it beside other experiences. He cannot avoid theology any more than he could avoid the vital question in the beginning.

An experience as infinitely rich and important to satisfy man's yearning sparks many different explanations. Men try to get hold of the core experience in words, and just as they think they have hold of it, they realize their expression is still inadequate. So they try again, either refining the original formulation, or, if that proves a dead end, taking a new approach to the problem.

The disciples had to articulate their experience at least adequately enough to enable other people to come to the experience. And they had to be able to talk to both their Jewish contemporaries and to the Greek world at large about this experience. How does it differ from other people's experience of life?

How is it better than other ways of looking at the world? What in the present world-view of a Greek or a Jew will help him understand the Christian experience? These are extremely difficult questions, and it is no surprise that the early years of the Christian faith are filled with attempted answers and vigorous refutations of what were considered wrong answers.

The birth of Christian theology

The New Testament evidences Christianity's earliest theologies throughout its pages. The Gospels represent profound attempts to articulate the experience of Jesus through a telling of his life. But the main source for nascent theology lies in the letters to the New Testament churches, and particularly the letters of the apostle Paul. Paul is, after Jesus himself, the most influential person in Christianity. Christian experience originates in Jesus and was given shape by the first Christian communities whose testimony forms our New Testament. Pre-eminent of the New Testament witnesses is Paul—the most influential and perhaps the greatest Christian theologian. He is represented in the New Testament far more than any other author, and his thought brought Christianity into the Greek world.

Paul enters a Christianity that still considers itself part of Judaism. He makes it a religion in its own right and translates its experience into language understandable outside of its original Jewish context. The civilized world of his day was that of Greece and Rome. Judaism was a small religion on the fringes of that world. Paul helped Christianity succeed by

translating his experience of Jesus into terms understandable to a citizen of the Roman Empire. Here
was his genius, and under his impetus Christianity
within three hundred years had become *the* religion
of the Roman Empire.

Paul began a task of theology which has continued
to the present day: translating the unique Christian
experience into terms intelligible to contemporary
man. Theology forms a bridge between a culture or
civilization and Christian faith. It is always an attempt, and being an attempt it can and does fail.
Naturally, today we can learn from 2,000 years of
theological practice. Christianity has been ham-
mered out on the anvils of countless cultures and
philosophies. But in its early days theology was a
dangerous enterprise. The young Church clung to an
experience which she was extremely anxious and
zealous not to lose. But every attempt at articulation
posed the danger of warping, distorting, or even be-
traying the original experience.

The Church soon gathered up those documents
which truly and perfectly transmitted and captured
her experience. These she made her safeguard, her
measure by which to judge any subsequent state-
ment. This collection forms the Bible. But inadequate understandings soon arose and in order to preserve her experience from distortion she was forced
to formulate expressions opposed to those which betrayed the experience.

Ultimate expressions of this kind are called
dogmas. Dogma is usually defined by the Church
when the truth of the experience is in danger of being
wrongly understood. It forms a corrective. It does not
add to the faith: rather it secures and preserves it.

The Church has the power and right to propound dogmas only because she is the recipient of that original Easter experience. The disciples, receiving the experience, conveyed it to others. Communities grew up which lived and thought their lives from within that experience. Through these communities, these churches, the unique Christian experience is passed on. Only they know and live it; only they can judge concerning it.

When the great crises arose in the early Church, the question was often solved through a council: a gathering of all Church leaders, the successors of Jesus' disciples. The council examined the problem and in prayer attempted to formulate a solution true to the faith which had been handed down to them. The conciliar decisions then became the decision of the entire Christian people. Often these dogmas were published in the form of a creed, and this creed served as a guide for interpreting the faith and the stories of Jesus.

> The Israelites did not indulge in the Greek love for abstraction which really gave birth to science, philosophy and theology (and with theology, of course, the creeds). The Israelite was primarily concerned with history, for it was in the events of history that Yahweh was revealed and known. If anyone asked an Israelite what he believed, he would recount the events of his saving history. The following passage from Deuteronomy 26:5-9 is the most famous "creed" of the Old Testament:
> My father was a homeless Aramean

who went down to Egypt with a small
    company
and lived there until they became
a great and powerful and numerous
    nation.
But the Egyptians ill-treated us,
    humiliated us
and imposed cruel slavery upon us.
Then we cried to the Lord,
    the God of our fathers, for help,
    and he listened to us
    and saw our humiliation,
    our hardship and distress;
and so the Lord brought us out of Egypt
    with a strong hand and outstretched
    arm,
    with terrifying deeds,
    and with signs and portents.
He brought us to this place
    and gave us this land,
    a land flowing with milk and honey.

In the New Testament writings we have
no fully developed creeds, but there are
passages in which we can see the early
Christian communities attempting to express their faith in concise, easily remembered phrases. When Paul argues with the
Corinthians about life after death, he
relies on an early creed which, like
Israel's "creed," is more concerned with
history than theology:

Christ died for our sins
    in accordance with the Scriptures;

he was buried,
he was raised to life on the third day,
 according to the Scriptures;
He appeared to Cephus
 and afterward to the Twelve.
Then he appeared to over five hundred
 of our brothers at once
 most of whom are still alive, though
 some have died.
Then he appeared to James,
 and afterward to all the apostles.
  (1 Corinthians 15:3-7)

Another fragment of a creed appears in 1
Timothy 3:16:

He who was manifested in the body,
 vindicated in the spirit,
 seen by angels;
who was proclaimed among the nations,
 believed in throughout the world,
 glorified in high heaven.

And yet another creed lies behind 1 Peter
3:18-22:

For Christ also died for our sins,
 once and for all.
He, the just, suffered for the unjust,
 to bring us to God.
In the body he was put to death;
in the spirit he was brought to life
and in the spirit he went and made his
 proclamation

to the imprisoned spirits
through the resurrection of Jesus
Christ
who entered heaven after receiving the
submission
of angelic authorities and powers,
and is now at the right hand of God.

 **The Church Praying**

The following creed is the most famous in the Christian Church. It was promulgated at the Councils of Nicea and Constantinople beginning in the year 325. It is called the Creed of Nicea:

We believe in one God,
    the Father, the Almighty,
    maker of heaven and earth,
    of all that is seen and unseen.
We believe in one Lord, Jesus Christ,
    the only Son of God,
    eternally begotten of the Father,
    God from God, Light from Light,
    true God from true God,
    begotten, not made, one in Being with the Father.
    Through him all things were made.
For us men and for our salvation
    he came down from heaven:
by the power of the Holy Spirit
    he was born of the Virgin Mary, and became
        man.
For our sake he was crucified under Pontius Pilate;
    he suffered, died, and was buried.

On the third day he rose again
in fulfillment of the Scriptures;
he ascended into heaven
   and is seated at the right hand of the Father.
He will come again in glory to judge the living and
   the dead,
and his kingdom will have no end.
We believe in the Holy Spirit, the Lord, the giver of
life,
who proceeds from the Father and the Son.
With the Father and the Son he is worshiped and
glorified.
He has spoken through the prophets.
We believe in one holy, catholic and apostolic
Church.
We acknowledge one baptism for the forgiveness of
sins.
We look for the resurrection of the dead and the life
of the world to come. Amen.

The Christian Prays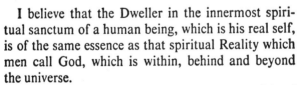

I believe that the Dweller in the innermost spiritual sanctum of a human being, which is his real self, is of the same essence as that spiritual Reality which men call God, which is within, behind and beyond the universe.

I believe that the nature of this ultimate spiritual reality, unknowable to the intellect, but knowable to the heart, is Love.

I believe that God was in Jesus the Christ, reconciling the world to himself.

          (F. C. Happold, **Prayer and Meditation**)

5

The Foundations of Christology

Of the many dogmas that have been formulated in the course of Christianity's long history, two are central to the Christian experience. These two dogmas define the very heart of Christian belief in Jesus and they are central to all the forms of the Christian faith. They answer the problem of Jesus' identity and his task: who was he and what did he accomplish?

The God who became man—incarnation

Every New Testament author wrestled with the question of Jesus' identity, and the issue was not finally and definitively solved until the Council of Chalcedon four centuries later. But the point at issue was more one of refinement and precision than a broad issue of Jesus' nature. The Christian community from Easter Sunday on has been convinced and has lived in the belief that Jesus was truly God without ceasing to be truly man.

The history of Israel was an education of a nation by God. Throughout their history, God prepares this people. He chooses them, delivers them from slavery, makes them a nation, gives them over to their enemies when they forsake him, and sends them prophets to call them back to him.

Finally, in the day of Jesus, God himself appears on earth—not as God but as a man like any man. The disciples who had lived with him lacked no conviction of Jesus' humanity. He grew tired. He became irritable. He could wax enthusiastic and grow discouraged also. Perhaps they sensed a special unique quality about him, but they never doubted that he was a man like them, and when he hung on the cross they never expected to see him alive again.

In Jesus' resurrection the disciples began to realize that merely to call Jesus a man did not accurately describe him. This man was in some significant way different from the rest of men. A mere man could not possibly conquer death. Not even Moses or the greatest prophets had escaped death. Only God would be able to conquer death. And as they prayed to God for guidance and wisdom and as they reflected upon Jesus and his words, they were led under God's guiding influence, under the inspiration of the Holy Spirit, to see that God had been working in Jesus in an entirely unique and astounding way. This man Jesus *was* God himself.

Certain incidents now made greater sense. This man spoke with authority; he dared do things no good Jew would presume to do, things seemingly against God's law. But if Jesus were God enfleshed in man, then his words *had* authority and were not blasphemous or presumptuous. His words would lead away from certain dead ends of the Jewish religion and back to a vital experience of God. The dis-

ciples knew that the words had divine authority when
Jesus' teaching was confirmed and sealed by his resurrection.

An early Christian story shows the concern of the
Christian community to define just how Jesus should
be appreciated in relation to God. The story tells of
the birth of Jesus and explains how his mother had
conceived Jesus through the power of God although
she was a virgin. However, the story of Jesus' virgin
birth is not concerned primarily with how Jesus was
biologically conceived. Instead this story wants to
say that Jesus was not adopted by God as his Son at
some point during Jesus' life or at the resurrection.
Jesus is God's Son from the moment of his conception in his mother's womb. On the other hand, Jesus
was completely human inasmuch as he was born
from a woman; not a God descended from the sky,
he partakes in our full humanity. This story of Jesus'
conception and birth later became a part of the Ni-
cene Creed. There we confess that he was "born of
the Virgin Mary by the power of the Holy Spirit and
became man." Again it is not the biology of repro-
duction that is of concern but what the story is saying concerning Jesus and who he is.

The doctrine of the incarnation (God-made-man)
lies at the center of Christianity. Jesus becomes the
focus because in himself he is both man and God. He
forms a bridge between man and God, reconciling
the two within himself and uniting God and man
always. His unique unrepeatable life forever elimi-
nates the possibility that either God or man can
completely be divorced or forget about or abandon
one another. As God became man to show himself to
us as love and forgiveness, so Jesus as a man accepted the invitation.

This doctrine cannot be totally explained: it remains on the plane of mystery. At the core, it says that the chasm between God and man exists no longer. Why should God have become man? No compelling reason—only out of love. But that it happened has been the witness of Christians everywhere from the world's first Easter.

When early Christians attempted to probe the mystery more deeply, to explain it more, they fell into many errors. The mystery holds together two statements. Jesus is truly a man, and Jesus is truly God. Jesus' divinity should not be overemphasized lest the man become a puppet or a mask. Emphasize his humanity too much and his uniqueness as God is lost. Nor should his personality be split: God one minute and man the next. He does not lie in his crib as an infant and from that crib contemplate how he made the world. Somehow in God's wisdom and power Jesus does not cease to be a man in every sense of our humanity even though he is truly God.

> Luke's account of the virgin birth is found in the first two chapters of his Gospel.
>
> Paul in his letter to the Philippians cites an ancient Christian hymn on the incarnation (Philippians 2:6-11).
>
> The hymn at the beginning of John's Gospel is the most sublime expression of the incarnation (John 1:1-8).

 **The Church Praying**

Father,
today in Christ a new light has dawned upon the world:

God has become one with man,
and man has become one again with God.
Your eternal Word has taken upon himself our
    human weakness,
giving our mortal nature immortal value.
So marvelous is this oneness between God and
    man
that in Christ man restores to man
the gift of everlasting life.

(Christmas Preface III)

The Christian Prays

Lord Jesus, the Way,
    the Truth,
    and the Life,
we pray,
do not let us stray from you,
    the Way,
nor distrust you,
    the Truth,
nor rest in anything else but you,
    the Life.
Teach us by the Holy Spirit
    what to do,
    what to believe,
    and where to take our rest.

(Desiderius Erasmus)

The death that won life — atonement

If Jesus is God-become-man, then his life, what he said, and what he did assume enormous importance. And the early Christians found in Jesus the culmination and the perfection of the Jewish experience of God. For thousands of years this people had been growing slowly to know God. The Old Testament is filled with glimpses of this God and of what he wants to say to us. It was his education and building of relations with men.

In Jesus the decisive breakthrough occurs. In this man are summed up all the teachings of Jewish history about the God who saves, all the prophets' words about a God who wants to draw near and to lead us toward him, all the longings of Israel's poets to sing and pray to, and celebrate worthily, this God, and all the writings of her wise men who showed Israel how to live in accord with God's infinite wisdom. Christians recognized Jesus as God's wisdom, his glory, his Word, even God himself. And his teachings about the love of God and man summed up and gave confirmation to the entire Jewish faith.

But Jesus went beyond the Jewish experience as well. And Christians saw in his death a unique and unparalleled act. It was unbelievable to the Jews that God would become a man and walk the earth with them, but that he would also die for them was absolutely unthinkable. This God shatters all conventions and expectations: he refuses to act as a God should.

In Jesus' seemingly senseless death, Christians soon saw a meaning. In the light of his resurrection and victory over death they perceived a more perfect repetition of the escape from Egypt. There God had delivered the slaves from their captivity. But in Jesus' death and resurrection God delivers all mankind from the slavery of sin and death. A guilty mankind nailed an innocent man to the cross. This man had come preaching love, and we could not stand his message. To stop him we killed him, pounding nails through soft flesh. We refused his love and preferred to live in silence, hating or at best tolerating one another. But the power of love was so strong that it broke through both the violence of our guilt and sin and the chains of death and the grave. Love won and freed us from the curse of our pride and isolation in spite of our obstinancy.

In the incarnation God broke through the barrier between himself and us by becoming a man. In Jesus' death and resurrection he led us into freedom, not from human masters, but from the greatest enemies: sin, which makes it impossible for us to live in peace with one another, and death, which continually tells us everything we do is in vain.

God broke through both barriers, and on the cross his love proved that his commitment to us can never fail, die or be broken. We are now at one with God through his death on the cross whether we are aware of the glorious news or not. The battle is won—love *has* conquered division and death. All that remains now is that all people everywhere become aware of this at-one-ment and come to experience the Christian joy.

The answer to our life's vital question is not a program of what we should do—it is the good news of what has already been done. Jesus slew death and broke the wall separating us from our true happiness. God's only adequate name is Love, and Jesus has brought love to us and made it possible to love one another because he has freed us forever from the enemies of love: sin, guilt, envy, anger, death.

It is impossible to understand the inner dynamics of the atonement completely. But whenever Christians have allowed the Easter experience to mold their lives, whenever they have taken to their hearts the resurrection stories, whenever they have entered into the Easter rituals, then they have found it possible to overcome the destructiveness of sin in their lives and live at peace with their fellow man; for them death has no longer held a fear. We are free right now; why then do we live as though we were still in chains?

> Acts 13:17-39 reports a speech by Paul on what Jesus accomplished.
>
> Paul's theology of the atonement reaches its apex in Romans 5:12-21.
>
> Colossians 1:21-23 contains a later Christian development of atonement theology.

 **The Church Praying**

Father,
when your children sinned
and wandered far from your friendship,
you reunited them with yourself
through the blood of your Son
and the power of the Holy Spirit.
You gather them into your Church,
to be one as you, Father, are one
with your Son and the Holy Spirit.
You call them to be your people,

to praise your wisdom in all your works.
You make them the body of Christ
and the dwelling place of the Holy Spirit.

                    (Preface for Ordinary Sunday VIII)

The Christian Prays

Jesus, for your name's sake,
do that which your name proclaims.
Jesus, pardon the pride that pained you,
and look upon the unhappy one
that calls on your tender name;
name of comfort,
name of delight, and to sinners,
name of blessed hope.
For what does your name mean, Jesus, but "Sav-
    ior?"
Therefore, for your name's sake,
be to me, Jesus,
a merciful Savior.

                           (St. Augustine of Hippo)

6

The Kingdom, the Power,

and the Glory

The coming of the Kingdom

The God of Israel had been a God of politics. He was the God of the marketplace and a God of armies. He had more intercourse with kings and prophets than with priests and temples. His first concern was a kingdom for his people; a temple where he himself might dwell was always a side issue in his eyes. He preferred justice to a neighbor over pious sacrifices. He was a God who spoke words, words and more words—a true politician.

Jesus' preaching continued his Father's emphasis upon politics. Like the prophets and John the Baptist before him, Jesus focused upon God's kingdom. The dream of the kingdom was now over two thousand years old. It was truly a battered and worn dream. Nevertheless, the kingdom was still expected and anticipated. John the Baptist spent his life convincing people that the kingdom was arriving soon. Jesus taught that the kingdom had already been inaugurated. The tiny seed had been planted that would eventually grow into a giant mustard tree where all the creatures of heaven would be able to nest.

The kingdom is the state in which God will be acknowledged as king. However, Jesus did not overly emphasize God's kingship or his role of judgment so much as his fatherhood. By calling God "Father" Jesus removed much of the impersonality from the concept of the kingdom.

If the kingdom is that state in which God is allowed to be our Father, then the kingdom is that state in which all other people are considered to be our brothers and sisters. Therefore the kingdom is that state in which we are ruled by the justice of love (that type of justice which prevails in a family) rather than the justice of law (that justice which prevails in the ordinary political state).

The kingdom is founded upon the forgiveness of sins and the healing of our bodies. In order for God's kingdom to come, all the hurts and injustices of man's kingdom must first be rectified. Jesus began this mission through his work of healing and the forgiveness of sins. It was the latter act that made him a heretic in Jewish eyes. Since only God could forgive sins, they felt that Jesus had blasphemed.

In a sense the kingdom of God announced by Jesus is not of this world. The kingdom and the world are incompatible with one another. The kingdom will replace the world. Jesus' understanding of the kingdom is tied up with his belief that the world will soon end. Once this order of things passes away, the kingdom will be able to appear with power.

We must not make the mistake of identifying the kingdom with any institution which exists in this world. The kingdom is here and now coming into the world, but it will not live alongside the world. The world must pass away to make room for the kingdom.

However, neither is the kingdom other-worldly. It is not a religious reality but rather a secular order. A true religion attempts to separate everyday life from a special life and time called sacred. There are some people, actions and things that are holy, while other people, actions and things are not holy but profane (their proper place is outside the temple, the holy place). Israel's God was never comfortable with this distinction we make between holy and secular, for he who was holy always crossed over the line into the secular. He entered history, meddled in politics, and finally put on human flesh. He continually transgressed the boundaries we had set up to keep the holy unpolluted.

Jesus did not recognize any distinction between the holy and the profane, between the sacred and the secular. To him all life was holy, and no part should be hidden from God. The Jews thought that they were being good Jews when they worshiped God with the prescribed sacrifices, but the prophets warned that God demanded not sacrifice but justice. Jesus condemned the religious men and women of his own day who made sure they said all the right prayers and did all the right "holy" things. They were censured because they lacked love and forgiveness for their brothers and sisters.

Jesus never speaks of God's kingdom in religious or churchy terms. Mostly he taught using parables or stories taken from everyday life. He told of a father who forgave his son, he spoke of a widow who badgered a judge until he finally relented, he cited the good shepherd who went after one sheep that was lost. If any of these stories sound religious today, it is only because for two thousand years they have been recited in our churches. However, the original images are far from religious. If we substitute modern images in the parables, such as replacing the shepherd by a farmer, we might regain some of the worldly sense of Jesus' original story.

For Jesus, religion is not what one does on the holy days in the holy places; religion is what we do everyday in the everyday places. In our work, in our love, in the people we live with ordinarily—there are the seeds of God's kingdom.

We Catholics may have some difficulty relating to this secular teaching of Jesus, for we associate Jesus with Church, and Church is where religion happens. Furthermore we think of God's kingdom as heaven somewhere in the sky. Thus we are sometimes shocked that the people of the Church should have anything to do with secular life. In the past it was unthinkable for priests and nuns to go to films or plays. They were to reserve their life for holy things. They lived apart in rectories, monasteries and convents so that they would not be contaminated by the world.

However, God's kingdom is not something in the sky. It will come here on earth in the middle of our cold, cruel, secular world—and it will not come through necessarily religious actions such as the lighting of candles and the praying of novenas. It will come through forgiveness of our neighbor, feeding the hungry, caring for the sick, and teaching the ignorant. If our prayers and candles do not lead us back to the marketplace and these "social" actions, then no matter how holy, they lead us away from God's kingdom rather than toward it.

We are not "of the world," for the world will pass away. Thus we cannot afford to be like the world— uncaring, unforgiving, unloving, interested only in ourselves. Through Jesus and his message we are able to judge that such a way of life is dead. We are "in the world" as seeds of the kingdom, and we must act in issues of concern. We must fight discrimination, prejudice, war, poverty, and disease in the name of the kingdom, for in Jesus' eyes the doctor and teacher are as holy as the priest.

The signs of the Kingdom

Jesus not only talked about the kingdom in his parables, but he also performed miracles. Now miracles create problems for a modern person, for how can we believe that all those miraculous things happened? It might be easier for us to believe Jesus if he had performed no miracles, if he had simply preached the kingdom. The miracles make him seem like a preacher who is also a magician.

However Jesus' miracles are not simply magical tricks. In fact we really should not even call them miracles. Let us instead refer to them as signs, for they are events which demonstrated to the people Jesus met that in this man the kingdom of God is present.

It is certainly a fact that Jesus effected cures both of physical disease and mental disturbances. He did this primarily not to show that he was God or even necessarily to help the individuals who were healed (although this was one important reason for curing them).

The healings proclaimed that the time prophesied by Isaiah had come. "The lame walk, the blind see, the lepers are made clean, the deaf hear, the dead are raised to life, and the poor are hearing the good news." The signs of Jesus point to the kingdom and describe that kingdom just as the parables do. In fact let us think of the signs simply as parables in action rather than parables in word.

The other signs of Jesus such as the walking on water, the calming of the storm, and the raising of Lazarus must be interpreted individually to determine whether they possibly go back to Jesus' life or whether they are stories told about Jesus in the early Christian communities in order to teach something concerning him. For example, the calming of the storm says that Jesus does the same things which the Israelites had attributed to Yahweh. Therefore this story is a confession by the early Christians that Jesus is indeed God just as Yahweh is. In these sign stories it is more important to determine the meaning of the story than to discover whether Jesus actually performed the sign as it is described. It is more important to realize that the story is a confession of Jesus as God than to ask whether he stopped a certain squall one day.

Two of Jesus' most famous parables are told beautifully by Luke. They are the parable of the good Samaritan (Luke 10:29-37) and the parable of the prodigal son (Luke 15:11-32).

Mark records three of Jesus' signs in succession in his Gospel—first the healing of the daughter of the Syro-Phoenician woman (Mark 7:24-30), then the healing of the deaf man (Mark 7:31-37) and finally the miracle of the loaves (Mark 8:1-10).

━━━━━━━ **The Church Praying**

Father,
let the light of your truth
guide us to your kingdom
through a world filled with lights
contrary to your own.
Christian is the name and the gospel we glory in.
May your love make us what you have called us to
   be.
   (Opening Prayer—Fifteenth Sunday of the Year)

The Christian Prays ━━━━━━━

Teach us, good Lord,
to serve you as you deserve;
to give and not count the cost;
to fight and not heed the wounds;
to toil and not seek for rest;
to labor and not ask for reward
save that of knowing we do your will
through Jesus Christ our Lord.

(Ignatius of Loyola)

The power of the kingdom

If Jesus was truly God working among us, why did
he retreat from the scene after his resurrection?
Would it not have been better for him to stay around
in order to make sure that his vision of God's kingdom was correctly implemented? With Jesus around,
everytime we ran into a problem we could consult

him and immediately have the discussion cleared up. Under such a system the last two thousand years would have been ample time to bring about the kingdom on earth.

However, God's kingdom is not a dictatorship with one master calling the shots and a number of little slaves carrying out the orders. We like to think of God in this way, but it is very demeaning to him. We are not slaves but children of the kingdom, and the kingdom will come in power through our lives and efforts worked in freedom.

We were left a legacy by Jesus—his vision of the kingdom. That vision now resides with us, but it must be applied and brought to life in our daily routine. The ideal words of Jesus must be translated into the practical actions of day-to-day survival. If Jesus is the architect of the kingdom, we are the engineers, the stonemasons, the road builders, the carpenters. We must carry the vision into blood and bones.

The vision left to us is not a dead blueprint. The vision of Jesus is alive and dynamic. It grows, it is creative of new life, it breaks all boundaries and will not be confined to static situations. This vision also has power. It has the power to transform our world and eventually to bring about the kingdom on earth. It has the power of God.

Christians have found that the best way to describe this living, powerful vision of Jesus is in terms of spirit. We say that the vision of Jesus inspires us, or that the Spirit of God comes into our lives. To say this, of course, is to say that the vision of Jesus is God himself.

The Holy Spirit is that experience of God which is most personal to us. The Spirit is the divine spark that illumines our lives. The Spirit is the vision of Jesus carried into daily living some two thousand years after Jesus himself. The Spirit is that magnet of God drawing us home to the Father through Jesus.

While Jesus was physically among us, the locus of divine power in our world rested in him, but now that his vision has been sent to the ends of the earth, the power of God and the center of divine activity is no longer localized. It is without boundaries of either geography or history. If we are drawn by the vision of Jesus, we are drawn by God the Spirit.

We Catholics did not place much emphasis upon the Holy Spirit until recently. Certainly we did not deny him, but we did not leave much room for him to work freely. We depersonalized the Spirit and enfeebled his power by speaking much of grace. As Christians we were acquisitors of grace. Grace flowed around us in the sacraments, and we tried to gather up and hoard as much as possible. Grace would bring us to heaven. We thought of grace somewhat crudely as liquid gold by which we could buy passage to salvation.

Let us instead look at grace in terms of power. There is no sense in hoarding power. Power is to be used in order to achieve something, and the power of Jesus' vision is to be used not to get to heaven when I die but to help in the coming of God's kingdom on earth.

Grace thought of in terms of liquid gold is static. We hoard it and therefore we can be passive toward life. Whatever happens, we will not be moved. We have our treasure and it is in a safe place. However, grace thought of in terms of power is dynamic and alive. It involves us in the world; it maneuvers us into the flowing stream of life.

Perhaps because of the long history of misunderstanding, it is time to abandon the old concept of grace for the more modern one of power. Moreover, we should realize that whenever we speak of God's power at work in our lives, we are speaking of the Holy Spirit.

The Spirit of God pervades Holy Scripture. It inspires the prophets (Isaiah 61:1-2) and it is part of their prophecy that on a future day the Spirit of the Lord will be poured out over all the earth (Joel 3:1-5).

In the New Testament John is the theologian of the Holy Spirit. In his Gospel Jesus discourses upon the Spirit on the night before his death (John 14:15-31; 16:4-15), and John describes the in-breathing of the Spirit after the resurrection of Jesus (John 20:19-23). Luke describes this same event which Christians celebrate on the feast of Pentecost in Acts 2:1-47.

The Church Praying

God our Father,
pour out the gifts of your Holy Spirit on the world.
You sent the Spirit on your Church
to begin the teaching of the Gospel:

now let the Spirit continue to work in the world
through the hearts of all who believe.
(Votive Mass for the Holy Spirit—Opening
Prayer)

The Christian Prays

Holy Spirit,
we pray to you—give us life,
as you breathed life and grace
into the soul of man in the beginning
and as you raised Jesus, our brother,
to life from the dead.
Give life and meaning
to the mortal body of his Church.
Remind us of everything
that he lived for.
Make us fire of your fire,
light of your light,
as the Son of Man, Jesus,
is light of the eternal light in you
and God of God,
today and every day,
for ever and ever.
Amen.

(Huub Oosterhuis, **Your Word Is Near**)

The glory of the kingdom

Unfortunately for all of the serious people of this
world, the God of Israel and Jesus is a very peculiar
and idiosyncratic God. He makes decisions and be-

comes involved in a very limited national history and in a humanly limited individual. He does things unbecoming to a God: he loses wars with other nations, and he gets himself nailed to a cross. Moreover, in choosing the chief sign for his coming kingdom, he has again made a choice which people might consider scandalous or at best another failure. For the glory of God's kingdom is seen on earth in his Church, and few people outside the Church can see the gloriousness for the grubbiness.

Yet it is the Church that is the sign of the kingdom. The Church is one of the signs of Jesus, for he created the Church. The Church's sole function is to point toward the kingdom and to show people what the kingdom is like. She does this by carrying on the preaching of Jesus and by being a place where healing, nourishment, forgiveness, and growth in love can take place. The Church is the gathering of all the people living out Jesus' vision.

However, the Church is not the kingdom. Heaven help us if it were. The Church is not even the seed of the kingdom planted in the world, although she certainly contains many seeds of the kingdom. No, the kingdom is much larger than the Church. The kingdom will include all of God's people—all men and women of good will, and not just Christians. Moreover, there may well be Christians who will not be part of the kingdom. Jesus said, "Not everyone who cries 'Lord, Lord' will enter the kingdom, but those who do the will of the Father."

Thus the Church is a sign of the glory of the kingdom. She is a sign that God's kingdom will be made out of the ordinariness of human flesh. She is a sign that the kingdom will be built out of our world, by common people with feeble talents who work and succeed only by the power of God.

Israel, of course, is God's first choice. She was the vessel of his glory, but often she was also the object of his wrath. Ezekiel's story of the two sisters demonstrates how bitter and terrible God's words to his glory could be (Ezekiel 23). Yet in spite of everything, after the bitterness there was always a promise of a new day when Jerusalem would shine in glory (Jeremiah 31:35-40).

John has Jesus pray right before his death for his disciples who would form the early Church (John 17). Luke describes this early Christian community in Acts 2:37-47, and an ancient Christian hymn concerning the glory of the Church is cited in Ephesians 1:3-13.

The Church Praying

God our Father,
in all the churches scattered throughout the world
you show forth the one, holy, catholic and apostol-
    ic Church.
Through the Gospel and the eucharist
bring your people together in the Holy Spirit
and guide us in your love.
Make us a sign of your love for all people,
and help us to show forth
the living presence of Christ in the world.
(Opening Prayer—Mass for Local Church)

The Christian Prays

Remember, Lord, your Church:
deliver her from all evil,
perfect her in your love
and gather together from the four winds
her people into your kingdom
for yours is the power and the glory forever.

(Ancient prayer found in the Didache)

Part III
The Rituals of
Christianity

Introduction: Conversion

from Passenger to Driver

The worship we offered in the garden of Eden was a worship of incense, candles and whispered sanctified phrases. It was, above all, holy and remote. It occurred at a holy time and was enacted in a holy place. For its service men were selected and set aside as priests. They performed the sacred action, and we the people joined ourselves to the action through them as best we could.

A well-known bus company in this country has the slogan: "Leave the driving to us." This was very much our situation in the old liturgy. The Church through the priests told us, "Come to Mass, and leave the action to us." Perhaps in the interests of ecology and economy it would be better for Americans to jump aboard mass transportation and forsake the individuality of the automobile. However, we Americans also know from experience that mass transportation is still not the most convenient or efficient mode of travel in a city, even though in visiting a great national park mass transportation or a guided tour might be the best way to see all the sights.

On a guided tour through a park, we use mass transportation because we are there to see the sights. Similarly, in the old Church the liturgy was like the guided tour. We were the passengers whom the priest led through the ritual actions and the seasons of the year. However, if our image of religion shifts from the park to the city we find that we need a different type of transportation. In the city we have to be able to go from area to area quickly and conveniently. In the modern city we often find that there is just no substitute for the automobile. Thus we are no longer passengers; we are usually drivers.

Today the shape of the liturgy, the mode of its performance, and its meaning to us have all changed drastically. Most of the change and confusion can be attributed to the shift in our role as the people. We are now no longer expected to be spectators; we are asked to become participants. We are no longer treated as passengers; we have been given drivers' licenses and the freedom of the road.

The priest is no longer the principal actor in the drama. Instead he functions more as a producer or director. He assists us in offering praise to the Lord. He has become our leader in prayer. He does not pray on our behalf; rather he directs, forms and leads our prayers. He has put away the uniform of the tour guide for that of traffic officer. He does not perform the sacred actions alone. The community as a whole re-enacts the great drama which gives meaning to our lives.

Since the liturgy has been restored to an action in which we take part rather than an action which we watch, it is necessary for us to change many of our attitudes about worship. We were accustomed to Sunday Mass as an occasion when we could be alone with our prayers, a time of peace and quiet. Now there is little chance for individual prayers during the *liturgy. Rather we must learn to pray together as a community. This is a new experience for us, and often we find it painful and bewildering. It is some- what similar to the adjustment period in marriage when the new husband and wife have to learn to live for one another rather than for themselves. Since the time for individual prayer during the liturgy is gone, we must find ways to make time for individual prayer in other parts of our lives, for although the liturgy is the center of our prayer lives, it cannot be the total expression of our prayer. The liturgy builds upon our individual prayer life, and if that prayer life is non-existent, it builds upon nothing.*

In the liturgy itself we must make an effort to join in the prayers, the singing, and the gestures. If possi- ble, we should volunteer for the different roles in the liturgy, such as reading, distributing communion, or singing in the choir. The liturgy is truly our action only if we make it so. Let us remember that the lit- urgy is our true school in Christianity. Just as in school we never learned anything by sitting on the sidelines, so now in the liturgy we shall never truly put on the vision of Jesus unless we make the effort to participate actively in our worship.

7

The Drama of Worship

Walk into Easter

Stories at best are only an invitation to enter into the Christian outlook; they make faith appealing but they cannot communicate it in all its richness. Stories appeal to us primarily as listeners. At best a story can compel us to enter into it, but only imaginatively: our body remains relatively uninvolved. While our mind enters the lands and vistas of the tale, our body remains seated in front of the storyteller, or holding a book in front of us, or watching a screen.

But the Christian experience works upon and transforms the whole person. We have to enter body and soul into the Easter morning event; like the apostles, we must be eye-witnesses to this event. Such witnessing is possible through ritual. Ritual is drama where we are actors rather than audience. In ritual we act out certain key dramas related to Jesus in order to bring Jesus, his outlook, his experience into our own lives. As Paul said, we "put on Jesus," we shape our lives, the story we tell, in accordance with Jesus' story.

Ritual involves worship. For most of us worship means going to church, saying our prayers or getting down on our knees. But these are only the externals of worship. We come closer to the true nature of worship if we think of it as admiration and imitation. When we find a person we admire, we want to incorporate something of that person into our own lives. Children imitate more consciously than adults. A small boy will often attempt to be just like his father. He will walk like him or talk like him; when he sits down in a chair he will cross his legs just like dad. He admires his father and he then copies and imitates him to capture in his own life what he admires.

This phenomenon persists in a more unconscious form throughout adulthood. We only grow and change by imitating a role until it becomes natural. If we admire Jesus and the way he saw the world, we want to incorporate into our own lives the manner in which he approached life. And we can do that through imitation and admiration. When we admire and attempt to copy Jesus we are worshiping him.

In ritual and worship we act out certain actions which help us to appropriate into our lives traits and qualities we find admirable in Jesus' life. Christians feel that only by assimilating themselves to Jesus can they be happy and fulfilled. If Jesus is truly God living as man, then his vision of life is the perfect vision; his way of dealing with his fellows and with God is the true way; his way of living leads to the fullest life, the life that death does not end.

Christian worship includes praise and adoration, thanksgiving and petition. All these activities bring the worshiper into closer relationship to God. We adore God because of his greatness, because of his love for us, because of his goodness—because in the last analysis he is God. We give him thanks for what he has done for us. We thank him for the beauty of the story he has unfolded in Israel and in Jesus. We thank him for the breathless awe we feel when we stand before his creation: the brightness of a sunrise, the majesty of a mountain, the silence of a remote pond, the dignity of a river. And we petition him for our own needs, the needs of all those dear to us, and for all people.

Christian worship is our school. Here we become acquainted with the stories and the person of God. Worship involves our response to God through adoration, thanksgiving and petition. But it also contains God's response to us: a reminder of what he has done in the past, and, in his sacraments, a making real and present his love and care for us today.

In worship we learn about God. If we had only the stories and dogmas we might think them true, but they would not touch us deeply, they would not change our lives significantly. God and his love for us would remain mostly an intellectual knowledge. We might realize that he loves us but we could not feel or experience that love. Nor would we be able to grow, deepen and mature in that love. For if love is to grow it must be experienced in all its vitality between the two lovers.

We might confess that God was a living, dynamic God but there would be no way for us to feel him alive in our own lives. In worship we do encounter the living God. We come to know him as we learn what he has done and as we experience what he is doing in our lives now. And finally, because we come to know him, we grow to love him and want to imitate him. And in the holy play of worship as we re-enact what he has done we bring into our own lives the experience of Jesus. And when we experience the world this way, when we see it through his eyes, have we not become like Jesus?

 **The Church Praying**

Hymn of Praise

Glory to God in the highest,
  and peace to his people on earth.
Lord God, heavenly King,
almighty God and Father,
  we worship you, we give you thanks,
  we praise you for your glory.
Lord Jesus Christ, only Son of the Father,
Lord God, Lamb of God,
you take away the sin of the world
  have mercy on us;
you are seated at the right hand of the Father:
  receive our prayer.
For you alone are the Holy One,
you alone are the Lord,
you alone are the Most High,
  Jesus Christ,
  with the Holy Spirit
  in the glory of God the Father. Amen.

Symbols: clusters of meaning

Jesus' life and teachings hold the key to living in and understanding the world. In this man lies the meaning of life, and this meaning is contained in certain symbols.

A symbol is a focus of meaning. It contains within itself a meaning. We cannot live without symbols and man could be defined as a symbolic animal. For he is an animal that seeks for meaning, lives for meaning and cannot exist without meaning. Anything that has meaning for humanity or says something to us is a symbol. Symbols include clocks, pictures, water, fire, a handshake, a kiss, and of course words themselves. Because symbols contain meaning within them they become centers of power.

We Christians are primarily concerned with certain core symbols connected with Jesus which we call sacraments. These sacraments contain symbols which concentrate so much meaning that they have the power to change our lives and to sustain us. This power is what we used to refer to as grace. It is primarily the power of meaning which gives purpose to our existence, and we name the power which transforms us by means of the sacraments the Holy Spirit.

Made meaningful in nature

Some things are symbols merely because we have agreed that they shall signify something. A stop sign brings us to a halt simply because our society has decided it should. Such symbols are more properly called signs and will not occupy our attention.

But other symbols carry an intrinsic meaning, not merely a meaning we have imposed upon it. A stop sign in itself carries only an arbitrary meaning. But water, fire, and the concept of "word" carry a meaning in themselves. True they have a meaning for us only because we seek meaning. But we have not given these symbols their meaning. Rather the meaning we find there resides in them already. Water means both life and death because we need it to live and we die from its lack or by drowning. But we have not imposed this meaning upon water; the meaning resides in the water simply by the nature of things.

Such symbols have a power in them: they bring to us a meaning beyond ourselves. Through these symbols we can enter into a relationship with our world: the world itself takes on meaning for us. Meaning is not limited to our minds and intellects but it can be found in the world about us. It is not just the case that we need to have meaning in order to live and so we impose it on our lives and our world. No, these great symbols of water or fire speak to us of a meaning that does not depend solely upon ourselves.

Christian rituals make use of our natural symbols such as fire, word and water. Christianity takes the natural symbols and builds upon them. It is an enrichment of our life: through our experience of Jesus we are made more human, we become more as God wishes us to be; we become more ourselves. All of us have some meaning in our lives, some meaning that derives from natural symbols. Who cannot feel reborn with the return of spring? The cold snows melt away and we await eagerly the first flush of green, the first color returned to a dead world. And gradually the world comes alive again until it bursts in an orgy of flowers and rainbow colors. Spring is a natural symbol, and people have always read that symbol as rebirth.

Made history in Israel

The natural symbols found both in nature and in human society (such as love and forgiveness) were taken up into Israel's experience of God. But in Israel the symbols assume a new quality as they are drawn into Israel's history. For Israel experienced God primarily in the events of her life and her history. In history she perceived the power of God working. The natural symbols were drawn into the historical drama. And because they became part of Israel's sacred history their natural power or potential for meaning increased.

Made flesh in Jesus

Jesus builds upon the religious experience of Israel. He took up into himself the diverse strands of Israel's insights and once again transformed them, enriching their meaning, making them more universal, bringing their power for us to perfection. In Jesus these great symbols, natural to man and made historical in Israel's experience, reach to the very heart of reality. Their meaning is purified and enriched to such a degree that they become powerful enough to transform our life. The different symbols group together in new relationships around the person of Jesus. They form and enrich themselves according to his experience. And they are then passed into the Christian community, where they are embedded in dramatic actions relating to Jesus. These symbolic dramas are so powerful in meaning, so able to transform the person who comes in contact with them, that they receive a new name: sacraments.

The encounter of sacrament

Through the sacraments humanity enters into the Christian experience. Through their drama and symbols it is possible for people to meet Jesus Christ at certain important crucial moments of their lives. These crucial moments are familiar to all of us; they are moments when the vital question often arises: moments when the everyday world recedes from our vision and suddenly we are face to face with the great mystery of life: moments of birth, of growth, of sickness and healing, moments of vocation and choosing a course in life. These are gifted moments when life can take on a strange mystery and beauty, when we are open to the possibility of a deep meaning in our life. At such times we are open to encounter Jesus and his vision.

These powerful sacramental actions have the ability to plunge us into Jesus and transform us into his likeness. They exist to mediate Jesus to us; they bring us into contact with him so that, just as in his own lifetime in Palestine, he is able today to infuse us with his message, heal our wounds both physical and spiritual, nourish us in the life we share with him, and build us into his body. One of Paul's primary images of the Church was the body of Christ. Jesus lives on in the Church which is the continuation of his life, his message, his ministry and his vision here on earth. The sacramental actions occur within his Church, and they are truly acts of the Church in the name of her Lord. The sacraments exist for the benefit of Christians, so that those living today can meet and be healed by Jesus just as the people of his day could.

But if the sacraments exist in the Church and for the Church, their power is meant for the entire world. Israel experienced God as the God of one nation; Jesus teaches us a God of all humankind. Jesus' mission of teaching and healing was for all people. Similarly every Christian enters into that mission.

The sacraments plunge people into Jesus' experience so that they may grow into him, be healed by him, and witness for him. But the sacrament does not end with the encounter. It transforms and heals so that Christians might be able to carry the good news of deliverance and healing to the rest of the world.

Although it is the source of his life, ritual for a Christian is never the end. Always he is sent forth from the sacrament commissioned to bring evidence and signs of his experience into the world. As the sacrament transforms the individual Christian into another Christ, so the Christian in turn receives the power and the commission to make Christ's presence felt in the world. Jesus did not exist for himself but for his fellows. If they would be true, Christians cannot help but live for their neighbor.

Israel's songs and prayers are collected in the book of Psalms. Some of the most beautiful and famous include Psalms 8, 19, 23, 51, 130, and 150.

Often Israel's prophets had to attack Israel's worship in the name of the Lord, since worship had degenerated into mere words and ritual. It had become divorced from right living (Isaiah 1:11-20).

Jesus continues some of these prophetic themes as he teaches his disciples how to worship the Lord (Matthew 6:1-18).

Finally we see how the worship of the Church on earth is united with the worship in the kingdom as we read the great Christian poem of Revelation (Revelation 19:1-10).

The Church Praying

You are God: we praise you;
you are the Lord: we acclaim you;
you are the eternal Father:
all creation worships you.
To you all angels, all the powers of heaven,
cherubim and seraphim, sing in endless praise:
   Holy, holy, holy Lord, God of power and
     might.
   Heaven and earth are full of your glory.
The glorious company of apostles praise you.
The noble fellowship of prophets praise you.
The white-robed army of martyrs praise you.
Throughout the world the holy Church acclaims
     you:

Father, of majesty unbounded,
  your true and only Son, worthy of all worship,
You, Christ, are the king of glory,
eternal Son of the Father.
When you became man to set us free
you did not disdain the Virgin's womb.
You overcame the sting of death
and opened the kingdom of heaven to all believers.
You are seated at God's right hand in glory.
We believe that you will come, and be our judge.
Come then, Lord, sustain your people,
  bought with the price of your own blood,
  and bring us with your saints
  to everlasting glory.

(Hymn of Praise)

The Christian Prays

Lord, you are great and greatly to be praised;
great is your power,
and your wisdom infinite.
We would praise you without ceasing.
You call us to delight in your praise,
for you have made us for yourself,
and our hearts are restless
until they rest in you.

(St. Augustine of Hippo)

8

Sacraments of Initiation
—Baptism and Confirmation

The sacraments of baptism and confirmation stand at the door to Christian experience. They introduce people to that experience by plunging them into Jesus' death and resurrection and then commissioning them to carry the Easter faith into the world.

Natural meanings

First we must examine the three natural symbols associated with baptism and confirmation: water, fire and oil. Each has a powerful natural meaning in itself which is infinitely enriched by association with Jesus and his experience.

Stand before the sea and think—of time and eternity, of power in storms and soothing life-bringing breezes. Look back into the past; before men or animals, before even fish or plants, there was the sea. Older than any living thing it is the source of our life. "The river is within us; the sea is all about us." What is our blood, our symbol for life, but a river flowing within us? We came from the eternal sea, and often we dream of returning to that same sea, of going down to the sea in ships or alone to be washed clean and rocked in motherly arms where we can forget the land and the life behind.

Water has always been a twofold symbol. Life emerged from the water, and it cannot survive if it does not continue to be nourished by water. Fishermen respect the sea, for it provides them a living; desert nomads search the wilderness for the water necessary to feed their flocks and quench their thirst.

But death also lurks in the waters. The drought brings disaster to the nomad and the farmer; the storm threatens to flood out the land-dwellers and capsize the fisherman's frail craft. The water that gave life is also capable of taking it away. We come and go in generations, we build bridges over the rivers, we run our water down great aqueducts, we erect cities and replace nature with technology. But the sea remains, unchanged, lapping the shorelines of our lives. And when we are gone and forgotten it remains what it always was.

Fire too carries life and death in itself. It brightens a winter room and provides warmth from the cold outside. It is an essential element in our cooking: no longer must we eat our meat raw. It is the source of our energy, the power behind our great advances. But like the sea it is a power often beyond our comtrol. It eats up forests and makes the night sky bleed in agony. We die of cold from its absence and from burns in its excessive presence. We have worshiped it as a god for its power, mystery and wonder, and we have cursed it as a demon and made it a symbol of hell for its pain and destructiveness. It both lights our darkness and darkens our life.

Oil is not as powerful a symbol as fire and water. But it has been almost universally used as a symbol for priesthood and the anointing of kings. Oil symbolizes something rich, pure and holy, something expensive. Many people use it to cleanse their bodies. Others use it to prepare their food. It is a base for expensive perfume, and it is often employed as a medicine for healing wounds.

Made history in Israel

These are the primary symbols of Christian initiation. Water and fire bring both life and death; oil anoints man and consecrates him, setting him aside for the high offices of priest and king. These symbols are all taken up into the experience of Israel. They play a vital role in Israel's encounter with God when they become embedded in history and help to mediate God's response to our dilemma, our vital question. Their meaning is purified and enriched in Israel's history and becomes less ambivalent.

God had freed Israel from the bondage of Egypt by leading her through the sea. The sea parted and the people walked on dry ground through its midst. Water became a primary remembrance of God's deliverance. Again, as the people were about to go into the land God had promised them, the river Jordan which formed the boundary stopped flowing so that they could cross over.

But water could also be an instrument of God's anger and vengeance. The Israelites in their songs often saw God manifest in the storms that built up out at sea and then came raging onto the mainland. They told the story of how once upon a time God decided to destroy humankind for its wickedness. He caused it to rain for forty days and nights, creating a flood which destroyed all but one holy man and his family.

Water was also the source of life and nourishment. After the exodus the people wandered in the desert and God provided water from a rock for their thirst. God gives not only freedom but life itself. In the Hebrew story of the first man and woman there is a description of paradise. From this paradise of God ran four rivers which flowed out over the earth and watered it. Later in her history when Israel was destroyed and carried off to Babylon the prophet Ezekiel had a vision of the future temple which God would build in a restored Israel. Flowing from beneath the temple were four rivers, rivers flowing from God, rivers of regeneration and purification and nourishment.

Fire too was intimately associated with the exodus. God guided the people in a pillar of cloud by day and a pillar of fire by night. In Moses' first encounter with this saving God, he spoke from a burning bush. In both instances fire is a symbol of God's saving act.

Fire is also a symbol for purification and sacrifice. Like her neighbors, Israel offered sacrifice to her God through burnt offerings. But gradually through the teachings of the prophets it became plain that God most desired the sacrifice of loyalty and obedience to his Word.

The prophets often describe their encounter with God, using fire imagery. Isaiah tells how, when God called him to be a prophet, he protested that he was not worthy. An angel descended with a burning coal and placed it in Isaiah's mouth to purify him to speak the Word of God.

Like her neighbors, Israel consecrated places to God by pouring oil over them. Later, when she became a nation with a king, she anointed the king as a symbol of his office. As her days of glory faded into the past she looked forward to the great leader God had promised: the Messiah, God's anointed, the "Christ" in Greek. Anointing was thus a symbol of kingship, and it signaled God's approval upon a man for the office he was to fulfill. Anointing was a commission: it made a man king or priest and gave him a function and duty within the community. The king and the priest were dedicated to God and would serve as his ambassadors and instruments on earth.

Made flesh in Jesus

These great symbols, natural and historical, were gathered up in the Christian community and submerged in the reality of Jesus where they again were transformed and took on ever more meaning and power. Jesus at the beginning of his ministry presented himself to John the Baptist to be baptized. The Jewish ritual signified that a person was sorry for their sins and that they intended to change and amend their life.

Through his death and resurrection Jesus infuses new significance into baptism. Now it becomes a participation in Jesus' own death and resurrection. People present themselves for baptism so that they may enter into the experience they have heard in the stories. They descend into the water and are submerged under the water which symbolizes death and the tomb. The old person dies and in their place rises a new person who has conquered death by being born into Jesus and putting on Jesus' experience of death and resurrection. The waters that take life also give life.

Israel had once passed through the water from slavery to freedom. God had chosen a people for his own and delivered them from their masters. Now in Jesus all can pass through the water from slavery to freedom. A new exodus is here, not only an exodus from physical chains and bonds, but a salvation from the slavery of divisiveness, sin and death. Rising from the watery grave, it is again Easter and we see now not with our old eyes but with the eyes of the risen Christ. We were not born for death, and now in baptism we have put on Jesus and his everlasting victory over death and destruction.

Before the sea parted, the people who stood on the Egyptian shore were merely a motley crew of escaped slaves. The people who stepped onto dry land after passing through the sea were a nation, bound together because of God's choice. No longer could they be strangers to one another: they were responsible for one another; their destiny was a common destiny.

The man who enters the font of baptism is an individual. Stepping out of the font afterward, he is part of a family, a new nation, a community, a Church. The early Christians saw themselves as the new Israel, called into being by God, incorporating all people. The Christian is not just an individual. In a real sense he is, first, part of a brotherhood, and he experiences God primarily in terms of his community. Baptism is the entrance into that community.

St. Paul speaks of baptism as "putting on Christ." When a man asks to be baptized he asks to participate in Jesus' experience. He wishes to live his life in a way similar to Jesus, to see the world as he saw it. In baptism the old self dies. The old life is renounced as the vision of Jesus is put on. Incorporated into the Lord the seeker enters into Christ's body. Paul calls the Church the body of Christ. Jesus is found today in the Church, in the group of people who have entered into his faith and his vision. There he lives and ministers today.

If in baptism we put on Christ, then in a very real sense we are what he is. He was God's Son, and by participation in him we too become sons and daughters of God. And if we are all sons of one Father in Jesus, then are we not brothers and sisters one to another? Jesus' preaching of the brotherhood of man is made real and concrete through baptism into his Church. We can no longer look out only for ourselves. A family or a nation places the obligation upon its members to live with one another, to help and care for one another. No longer can I see another man's sorrow and shrug it off because it does not affect me. It *does* affect me because that man and I are bound together and I have a responsibility toward him as I do toward a brother.

Finally baptism is a rebirth. It allows us a new start in life. If we are born into Christ in baptism, then the old man, the man of dissension, selfishness and greed dies. We have all sinned, done what we know is wrong. But in baptism our sins and failings are forgotten. They are washed away in the water and we are cleansed; freed from the chains of our past we can begin again. We can make the kind of life we want, the kind of life we have chosen in Jesus. No longer do we have failure, sin and death hanging over our heads, threatening our existence at every point. We have seen the sun rise over the tomb on Easter morning. A man clothed in brightness has pointed out the highway toward the city built on Love.

Encounter with God

In the sacrament we encounter Jesus at a particular point in our life. Receiving the sacrament we enter into his experience. But there is nothing magical. Christians grow old like all people and finally die. Nor are they exempt from the quarrels, divisions, strife and sin that inflict everyone. The Church's history shows she has always been composed of sinners. Baptism does not magically grant us immortality or free us from our often inadequate and sinful selves.

But neither is baptism a mere formality, like an initiation into a fraternity. In baptism a Christian truly is reborn. He is incorporated into Christ's body and forever belongs to Christ. But this gift of a new life and a new vision must be used. We receive the vision in baptism. But we spend the rest of our lives growing into this vision, conforming our will to Christ's will, our love to his.

In baptism we are given not only the gift of Christian experience but the power to utilize the gift and mold our lives in conformity with it. Many of us have felt the power present in a sunrise or sunset, the power of a poem, of a flower, of spring. In Christ man's natural symbols are gathered up and transformed. They become more gifted with meaning, more powerful, more able to transform us into Christ's image if we only open ourselves to them.

The power we receive in Christian initiation is the power of the Holy Spirit. The Spirit comes to dwell within us; our bodies become, as Paul says, "temples of the Holy Spirit." In the life of the Spirit within us we are opened to the new world of Jesus. Through the Spirit our lives are ordered around meaning, and we experience the freedom and liberating exhilaration that come from knowing a purpose in life.

Jesus has given his Church the sacraments as the very sources of his presence within her. They sustain and give life to the Church, and she builds her whole existence around them: they are the air she breathes, the food she eats. As God became man in Jesus, so now through the breath of the Spirit all the universe is taken up into Jesus. Through the Church's sacraments—those powerfully exploding symbols which mediate the experience of Jesus—the Holy Spirit seizes our hearts and enables us to enter into the vision of Jesus. Whenever a sacrament is celebrated in his community, Christians have his promise that Jesus will be present and that the Holy Spirit— God's power to transform our lives with meaning— will be working and given in this holy action. The sacraments of initiation bestow the Holy Spirit— Christ's vision and the power to enter this vision. But if the gift is to be assimilated so that it may transform us, we must cooperate in the process. Sacra-

ments do not fail because they do not effect what
they claim. They fail only because we do not allow
their power to transform us.

For a Christian, water carries not only its natural
and Old Testament meanings. Water is a symbol for
Jesus Christ himself. He is the water that truly
quenches our thirst for knowledge. He is the water
able to cleanse us from our wrongs, our selfishness,
our fears, our sins. His is the healing water with the
power to bring us through the waters of death, to
heal our wounds, to give sight to us who were blind.

He is also our light, our fire, our candle. St. John
calls him the light of the world. The light came into
the darkness, but the darkness did not understand it.
Nor could the darkness overcome it. The light illumines every man who comes into the world.

Every year as Christians celebrate the great feast
of Easter, an Easter fire is kindled before the
Church. The fire is a symbol for Jesus and his victory over the darkness of the grave. All take their candle and light it from the fire. Then everyone proceeds into the darkened church. Dark death is
overcome as the light spreads from candle to candle,
from Christian to Christian. Christ's light is ablaze
in hundreds of candles; the one man who conquered
death has made it possible for the whole world to
walk in his light, to carry his light into the darkness
of their lives and to dispel that darkness.

The early Christians celebrated baptism during the
Easter Vigil. On the night when Christ broke the
bonds of death they relived that event in baptism.
Before the great Easter candle, the pillar of cloud
and fire for the new Israel, the convert passed
through the waters of death and arose to life in

Christ. He was then given a new white robe as a sign of his new purity and innocence. Then a candle was presented to him. Lit from the paschal candle, it was a sign for Christ's light now in him. Finally he was anointed with oil to signify his entrance into Jesus' kingship and priesthood.

Conversion from initiation rite to sin bath

In the earliest days of the Church the sacrament of baptism concluded with the anointing with oil which we now call the sacrament of confirmation. At first all Christian converts were adults, but soon these Christians had children. A problem then arose as to whether the children should be baptized immediately or should grow up and then request baptism. The community decided that their children should be baptized. They could not make a decision for the faith as an adult could, but they were born into a Christian home, and their parents would raise them in the faith. So the body of Christ now included children who could grow up physically and spiritually in that body. As Europe became Christian, soon most baptisms were of children, and it remains so today.

However, a child cannot be expected to carry on his Christian mission and ministry. He is a passive Christian, receiving rather than giving. Therefore, as infant baptism became more predominant, the ceremony of anointing was separated from it.

Unfortunately the practice of infant baptism in the Western Church has given rise to some serious misconceptions centering around the idea of sin. When an adult is baptized and begins a new life, we Christians say that his sins are forgiven in the rite of baptism. The new meaning that the vision of Jesus brings to our lives shows up our past behavior as selfish and uncaring. Certainly there have been times when we did wrong. We knew what was right but we refused to act rightly. However, Jesus said that by entering into his vision we can start again, without any old wrongs hanging over us. Thus in addition to admitting a person into the new community of Jesus and conferring the vision that is the Holy Spirit, baptism also washed away a person's past sins.

When baptism became predominantly a sacrament conferred upon children, the concept of sin changed significantly, and the term "original sin" entered the picture. The average adult has plenty of sins to be forgiven in baptism, but does a child have sins for which he needs pardon? Theologians had spoken of an original sin which is not an action. We do not commit original sin. Rather original sin is a description of our innate tendency to be attracted toward evil and wrong. The theologians said that baptism removes the taint of original sin, and we can see that by admitting the person into the community sharing Jesus' vision, baptism puts the person within a different environment, giving him a new vision which draws him toward good rather than evil. Supposedly a child raised in a Christian environment should not be under the sway of our natural tendency toward selfishness; he should be removed from the influence of original sin. Obviously such is not the case—the Christian community is filled with sinners—but that is not the fault of Jesus' vision; it is the fault of human weakness and our own disbelief in Jesus.

Over the years Christians came to consider baptism primarily as the sacrament washing away sins and removing one from the influence of original sin. No longer was baptism principally the means of entrance into the Christian community and the vision of Jesus (although it was still considered that too). However, once the main emphasis was placed on sin and its forgiveness, it was a mere step to think of baptism in terms of making a person acceptable to God.

Certainly sinners are not acceptable to God. Thus if a person was to be saved—if he was to come into God's presence—he had to be baptized. Now this is a perversion of Jesus' vision never taught by him or officially by the Catholic Church. Nevertheless many Christians have believed it. This distortion makes the Church, which is the sign of the kingdom, into the kingdom itself. Then baptism which initiates a person into the Church becomes an I.D. card enabling one to enter the kingdom. Once we mistake the Church for the kingdom, we realize that we must baptize everyone we can. Otherwise how can they be part of the kingdom?

Officially in the Catholic Church there were always other ways to enter the kingdom than through baptism by water, but unfortunately we also called these other ways baptism. Thus the confusion between the Church and the kingdom was perpetuated. These other ways were known as baptism of blood and baptism of desire. If someone was martyred for upholding the principles of the faith before being baptized, the Church considered that person as baptized by blood for the simple reason that many of the early followers of Jesus were martyred for their beliefs. Also, if someone who wished to become a Catholic died before being baptized, or who tried to live a good life even though he had never heard of Jesus or desired to become one of his followers, the Church held that such a person was considered to have received baptism of desire. Thus the Catholic Church always taught that there were many people who would be in God's kingdom who were not formally affiliated with Jesus' Church.

But then the Church became hung up in her requirements for the kingdom. What about the little children who did not yet know the difference between right and wrong? Could they enter the kingdom if they died before the age of reason? Many in the Church thought that they couldn't, and that in the case of a child the only way to enter the kingdom was through baptism by water or blood; any other children who died could not enter the kingdom. This belief generated in turn the creation of a special place—limbo—where these left-out people could exist.

Today limbo has been itself relegated to limbo. We realize now that baptism governs entrance into the Church and not into the kingdom of God. We presume upon the mercy and love of God to ensure that all little children who die are in his presence. After all it was Jesus who rebuked the disciples when they tried to keep the children from him.

The Church Praying

*Father of all consolation
from whom nothing is hidden,*

you know the faith of these parents
who mourn the death of their child.
May they find comfort in knowing
that you have taken him (her)
into your loving care.

(Prayer from funeral for a child
who has died before baptism)

When a child is baptized today, we celebrate its entrance into our larger Christian family. We as the Christian community accept it into our care, and we promise that as it grows in our midst we shall share with it the wonderful stories of Jesus as well as the Spirit of Jesus who lives in our hearts. For if this child grows up in such a family it will be sheltered from the tendencies toward sin, and it will grow up as a pilgrim toward the kingdom and as a sign for its fellows that the day of the kingdom has already dawned.

Significant texts on baptism are found in Matthew 3, John 3:1-21, John 4:1-42, and Colossians 2:6-17.

 **The Church Praying**

From the Baptismal Liturgy

Father, you give us grace through sacramental signs,
which tell us of the wonders of your unseen
power.
In baptism we use your gift of water,

which you have made a rich symbol of the grace
you give us in this sacrament.
At the very dawn of creation your Spirit breathed
on the waters,
making them the wellspring of all holiness.
The waters of the great flood you made a sign of
the waters
of baptism, that made an end of sin
and a new beginning of goodness.
Through the waters of the Red Sea you led Israel
out of slavery,
to be an image of God's holy people,
set free from sin by baptism.
In the waters of the Jordan your Son was baptized
by John
and anointed with the Spirit.
Your Son willed that water and blood should flow
from his side
as he hung upon the cross.
After his resurrection he told his disciples:
"Go out and teach all nations, baptizing them
in the name of the Father and of the Son and of
the Holy Spirit."
Father, look now with love upon your Church,
and unseal for her the fountain of baptism.
By the power of the Spirit give to the water of this
fount
the grace of your Son.
You created man in your own likeness: cleanse
him from sin
in a new birth to innocence by water and the
Spirit.

We ask you, Father, with your Son to send the Holy Spirit upon the water of this fount. May all who are buried with Christ in the death of baptism rise also with him to newness of life. Amen.

The Christian Prays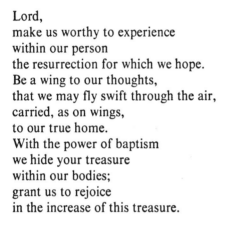

Lord,
make us worthy to experience
within our person
the resurrection for which we hope.
Be a wing to our thoughts,
that we may fly swift through the air,
carried, as on wings,
to our true home.
With the power of baptism
we hide your treasure
within our bodies;
grant us to rejoice
in the increase of this treasure.

(St. Ephrem)

Christian Mission

The ceremony of anointing, which in the earliest days was a part of baptism, symbolized the Christian's witness and ministry to all of God's creation. Nowadays it is postponed until the child has grown into adulthood and is ready to undertake the duty of witnessing. It has become the sacrament of Christian maturity and is known as confirmation. Confirmation today is thought of by most Christians as a sep-

arate sacrament. However, its purpose, the commissioning of the Christian to show his faith to the
world in his life and actions, is really only the completion of what was begun in the baptismal action.
The two sacraments must be seen together.

Oil was used in Israel in the ceremonies for coro-
nation and the ordination of priests. Jesus was the
true king, not only of Israel but of all peoples. He
was the true priest, for he mediated between God
and man. The baptized person enters into Christ and
assumes his mission and ministry. Christians are a
royal people, God's chosen people, a priestly people.
It is our ministry to unite the world, to build a community of love in the community of man.

Through the anointing with holy oil Christians are
ordained and receive a mission to carry Christ's light
to the rest of mankind. They must minister to their
fellows, teach them the good news, heal their wounds
and quarrels, free them from physical and spiritual
bondage, and bring them out of darkness into light.

Confirmation is also very intimately related to the
gift of the Holy Spirit, for it is the Holy Spirit of
God dwelling in our hearts as Christians who inspires us in our lives, who gives us the courage to
risk love, and who breathes into us our zeal for justice and mercy. The Holy Spirit keeps the vision of
Jesus fresh in the world. Furthermore, since confirmation focuses upon the Christian's mission, it is
also called the "seal of the Spirit" or "the confirm-
ing of the Spirit." However we must not make the
mistake of separating by too great a period of time
the moment of baptism from the moment of confirmation. Baptism initiates the action which finds
completion in confirmation. In spite of a separation

in years, these two moments are part of the same arc. When we say that the gift of the Spirit is given in confirmation, we do not mean to imply that in infant baptism there is no gift of the Spirit. We cannot make hard and fast distinctions between these two sacramental moments. What we can say is that in infant baptism the Christian community focuses primarily upon the child's reception into its midst and promises to nurture and support the child in the vision of Jesus. In the celebration of confirmation the community celebrates the young Christian's coming of age and growing maturity in the Spirit. We celebrate with the young persons as they begin their life as ministers of the good news of Jesus. Naturally when we celebrate the entrance of an adult into the Christian community we bring together the moments of baptism and confirmation into one action just as the early Christians did.

Every sacrament exists not only that a person may experience Jesus, but also that they may carry the fruits of that experience into the world. The Church exists only for the sake of the kingdom, and the moment of confirmation brings into high relief this experience of Christian living for others. For in confirmation, unlike the other sacraments, nothing is received for the recipient alone. Instead the recipient is sent out to give gifts to the world. Christians live for others, not solely for themselves. Their model is a man who laid down his life for his friends.

In the Bible we often hear of the Holy Spirit coming upon a prophet in order to speak through him (Isaiah 42:1-3) and we also hear prophecies which Christians have read to refer to Jesus in which the Holy Spirit radiates forth from a mere man (Isaiah 11:1-4).

Luke in Acts 19:1-6 shows Paul distinguishing John's baptism from baptism in Jesus which bestows the Holy Spirit. Paul himself has several important texts on the Spirit, including Romans 8:14-17, Romans 8:26-27, and 1 Corinthians 12:4-13.

 **The Church Praying**

All powerful God,
Father of our Lord Jesus Christ,
by water and the Holy Spirit
you freed these candidates from sin.
Send your Holy Spirit upon them
to be their helper and guide.
Give them the spirit of wisdom and understanding,
the spirit of right judgment and courage,
the spirit of knowledge and love,
the spirit of reverence in your service.

(Prayer for the imposition of hands)

The Christian Prays

May it be, Lord Christ,
that our words
which bespeak your glory,

shall be confirmed
by signs and deeds,
and that we may at last be perfect,
you cooperating in all our words and works,
for yours is the glory of both words and works.

(Theophylactus)

9

Sacrament of Christian Nourishment and Growth — Eucharist

The gift of new life and vision which Christians receive in baptism and confirmation must be nourished if it is to grow and transform us. Just as our bodies need physical nourishment to grow to adulthood, so we need spiritual nourishment as well. The Mass or eucharist is the source of this nourishment.

Meal and Word

The eucharist is built upon three symbols: word, wine and bread. Bread and wine, the fundamental foods of many peoples, symbolize food and drink. Bread is the mainstay for many people for whom meat is a luxury. It keeps them alive: without it they would die. It does not occupy such a central place in our own diet, but memories of bread's importance linger in proverbs such as: "Bread is the staff of life."

Wine too in many cultures assumes an importance that it does not have for us. It forms the normal dinner drink, but it also carries festive connotations.

Being alcoholic, it lifts the spirits, makes conversation easier, and adds zest to the meal. It has the ability to enliven an otherwise ordinary meal; it is a symbol for rejoicing and feasting.

The meal itself has great significance for humanity. A true meal is not just a means of nourishing the body. Meals are to be savored and enjoyed. They provide relaxation and enjoyment after a day's work. Mealtime is a time set aside to enjoy the earth's food and to share the companionship of others close to us. We share ourselves with one another in conversation, fellowship and gentle humor. Our true model for a meal should be a family-style Thanksgiving dinner when the meal becomes an event rather than the quick bite grabbed or the drab fare gulped to stay alive.

The third eucharistic symbol is the word. Consider the miracle of the word. Words make us men, different from all other animals. We are animals who think and believe and hold ideas we are willing to die for: all because of the word's power.

The power of the word can heal a breach between men: "Forgive me, I'm sorry." It can make two people one: "I love you." It can carry us by images, stories and poems to places we have never been. Through slander and anger it can destroy our society with one another. Through philosophy and science it makes possible those wonders that our ancestors scarcely dreamed of. Such is the power of the word.

Remembering in Israel

Israel recognized the power of the word, but for Israel the word was primarily God's Word. In the beginning God had but to speak a word and the universe came into being. God's Word was in the Law which he made with Israel. He promised to make them a nation if they kept his Word. And later his Word blazed forth from the prophets as they brought God's judgment upon a people who had ceased to heed the Word. In her wisdom literature Israel studied God's purpose in history to find his Word for the living of their lives. They saw that God's wisdom comes forth from him to enlighten men in his ways.

But in addition to God's Word Israel was diligent in remembering his deeds which had brought her into existence. Each year she celebrated the feast of Passover in memory of her passing over from the bondage of Egypt into her freedom as God's people. She ate unleavened bread in remembrance of the flight when her ancestors had to eat unleavened bread because they could not stay in one place long enough to bake leavened bread.

The family ate a lamb in remembrance of the lamb's blood which the Israelites had splashed over their doorways so that God would pass over their houses on the night he struck dead the first-born of the Egyptians. Israel was saved by that lamb's blood.

And she drank wine in celebration and thanksgiving for what God had done for her, bringing her out of slavery and giving her a land of her own. Through the ritual meal Israel relived down through the centuries her exodus. She made it present again each year in the songs, stories and above all in the eating of the meal itself.

Ritual is a play, a game. We open ourselves as we do in a game. We enter into the events we are celebrating; we put them on, and for the duration all sense of daily time disappears. When we play a game we are not aware of time's passing. Our imagination takes over and for a moment we escape the clock and our present surroundings. We enter another world, a sacred timeless world. We are like little children playing at being grown up—for the duration of the game we are grown up. In ritual, present time disappears and we participate in the original event. We put on the vision our ancestors had and we rejoice that God has delivered us. In acting out the sacred game the past becomes alive for us and we are united with those men of long ago. We bring their experience to life in our own lives.

The Passover of Jesus

The night before he died Jesus celebrated the Passover meal with his disciples. But in doing so he gave the meal a new meaning so that when in the future his disciples celebrated this meal they would primarily remember Jesus rather than the old exodus.

Jesus took bread into his hands, and when he had given thanks to God he broke it and gave it to his disciples, saying, "Take and eat. This is my body." When supper was over he took the cup of wine. Again giving thanks he blessed the cup and passed it to his disciples, saying, "Take and drink. This is the new covenant, shed in my blood. It will be poured out for you and for everyone so that sins may be forgiven. Do this in memory of me."

Bread, the staff of life, our bodily food, is taken up by Jesus and made into his body—given to us as food so that we might grow into him. The festive wine becomes his blood shed on the cross—now made the drink that unites us to him. This simple action becomes the Christian Passover—our remembrance of Jesus' work. How God himself became a man and died on a cross so that all men might live— this is what we remember. We remember a new exodus from sin and death into everlasting life. And in our action of remembering, Jesus' vision grows in its power over our lives. In the frequent remembering of this meal our lives are gradually transformed by the power of the Holy Spirit, and the vision of Jesus begins to guide our existence and provide meaning. We celebrate a new freedom as sons and daughters of God.

This simple communion makes present for us the act of our salvation. We remember Jesus, his death and resurrection, and through the holy game of the meal, Jesus in the form of bread and wine gives himself up for us. He becomes food which nourishes us and brings us into eternal life. In the mystery of this celebration we are present on the hill of crucifixion and before the tomb on Easter morning. Time stops, and for the duration of the rite we live at the same time as the original events. Just as once on the cross, so now Jesus gives himself so that men might not die but live.

Christian eucharist

At first the eucharist was celebrated in homes, but as Christians were driven out of the synagogues, and as the Christian communities became larger, they began meeting before dawn on Sunday to celebrate the Lord's resurrection. They adopted the first part of the service from the synagogue: it consisted of prayers, songs and readings from the Scriptures. Then they celebrated the eucharistic meal. So arose the basic form of Christian service still used today.

The liturgy of the Word as the first part of the Mass is called is a celebration of the works of God through prayers, songs and readings. From the beginning Christians have seen Jesus as God's Word to man. Jesus is the perfect expression of man: in this man God has given all men an example and exemplar. If we are distinguished from the animals because of our words, then it is only natural that God should communicate himself to us in the form of the Word which was Jesus.

God is encountered today primarily through his sacraments: creation made transparent to let him shine through into our lives. But the sacramental symbol is never alone: it is always made fully human through God's accompanying Word. Christianity's stumbling block is that God has taken upon himself his creation in order to express himself. Water, bread and wine fully communicate God to man. The God who went so far as to become man also deigns to use human language to express himself. Human speech has been made divine, inadequate as it is. Sacraments are not speechless. They communicate through the senses, but through the Word they reach the core of our humanity also.

In the action of the eucharist the symbols of bread, wine and word are combined to create a vehicle of praise to the Father. The Greek word "eucharist" means "thanksgiving," and it is our giving thanks that forms the central and most important element in the eucharist.

Unfortunately in our past the moment of consecration was singled out as the most important element of the Mass. Lately it has become popular to consider the moment of communion as the most important element. But these are only isolated moments in a continuous action. They are important— very important—but we should not consider them the principal reason for celebrating the eucharist.

In the eucharist we give thanks by uniting ourselves to Jesus. We participate in his act of thanksgiving the night before he died. We offer ourselves in union with him as a thank-gift to our Father for all the goodness he has blessed us with. And we offer this gift of ourselves and our lives in unity with one another through the power of the Holy Spirit. In Jesus' eucharistic action and its constant remembrance in the Christian community—Jesus selflessly giving his life for us—we have the model for living our own lives as Christians.

The Church Praying

Priest: The Lord be with you.
People: And also with you.
Priest: Lift up your hearts.
People: We lift them up to the Lord.
Priest: Let us give thanks to the Lord our God.
People: It is right to give him thanks and praise.

Priest: Father, all powerful and ever-living God,
           we do well always and everywhere to give you thanks
           through Jesus Christ our Lord.

At the Last Supper,
as he sat at table with his apostles,
he offered himself to you as the spotless lamb,
the acceptable gift that gives you perfect praise.
Christ has given us this memorial of his passion
to bring us its saving power until the end of time.

In this great sacrament you feed your people
and strengthen them in holiness,
so that the family of mankind
may come to walk in the light of one faith,
in one communion of love.
We come then to this wonderful sacrament
to be fed at your table
and grow into the likeness of the risen Christ.

Earth unites with heaven
to sing the new song of creation
as we adore and praise you for ever:

People: Holy, holy, holy Lord, God of power and might,
heaven and earth are full of your glory.
   Hosanna in the highest.
Blessed is he who comes in the name of the Lord.
   Hosanna in the highest.
                    (Preface II for Holy Eucharist)

A journey of words and actions

The eucharist is the center of all Catholic worship. All the other sacraments of the Christian faith either point toward it or flow from it, and the Christian community often celebrates the other sacraments within the context of the eucharist.

Although the eucharist is celebrated daily in every Catholic church, Sunday is the principal day of worship. Christians gather together every Sunday to commemorate that first Sunday when Jesus broke the bonds of death. We come together as a community in order to share with one another our commitment to the vision of Jesus and to grow in that vision. Catholics have a very strong tradition of attending the eucharist which makes us a people and defines who we are. Without the eucharist at the center of our religious life we would no longer be Catholics. Indeed a Catholic may be defined as one who tries to attend the eucharist every Sunday.

The practice of Sunday Mass was considered so important that it was made one of the precepts of the Church and became in our eyes equal to the ten commandments. To miss Mass on Sunday or on a holiday of obligation was a mortal sin. The Church meant by this precept to emphasize the importance of the Sunday eucharist. Unfortunately the precept is often understood with the wrong attitude.

God does not sit in heaven just waiting until for some reason or other we miss Mass on Sunday so that he can damn us. The Church says we should attend Mass every Sunday simply because that is the least a member of Jesus' community should do in order to maintain his good citizenship. But if we are sick, if we have to work on that day, or if it would be a real hardship to attend Mass on a certain Sunday, there is no need to worry that we are thrown into mortal sin.

Further, our mere physical presence at Mass is not what the Church encourages through her precept. If I go to Mass merely to chalk up another Sunday in the great heavenly ledger, then it is worth nothing. If I go to Mass and fail to participate in the worship, if I go simply because I have to put in an appearance, if I go and fail to pray to the Father or attempt to share the vision of Jesus through the readings, the homily and the great thanksgiving prayer, I might as well not go. It is a waste of time. It is as sinful as not attending Mass at all.

Today many Catholics complain that the Mass has lost its meaning. It used to be one quiet hour a week for prayer. But now the Mass seems as hurried, confused and cluttered as the rest of the week. This description of our experience is true. We should feel somewhat ill at ease with the new liturgy. It is a brand new experience for us, and we have to reform all our old habits of prayer. The old liturgy provided a great amount of time for our private prayers and devotions, but we were not really part of that liturgy. We used the liturgy as a background to our private prayer life. Today the Church calls us to continue our private prayer life—but to do it in private.

However, the Church also calls us to enrich our prayer life with the depth of the public prayer of the official liturgy. To do this well we shall have to learn how to pray together as a people. Until we learn to do so, the liturgy will seem cluttered and unprayerful.

If we can develop a liturgical prayer life, our religion will take on more significance and meaning, and the liturgy, far from being an hour of distraction, will become an hour of growth and deepening in the Spirit of God. If the liturgy has lost meaning for us, it is not the fault of the Church or her changes. She has remained faithful to the Spirit of Jesus. She has undertaken a painful process of reform in order to enable each Christian more easily to assimilate the vision of Jesus. If the liturgy continues to be meaningless, we are to blame for not caring enough to educate ourselves and to change some old and not so good habits.

Another of the Church's precepts with regard to the eucharist raises further problems—the precept of the Easter duty. The Church said that in order to remain a Catholic in good standing one should receive communion at least once a year during the Easter season. However that precept was usually taught differently. We were told that we had to go to confession and *communion, and many Catholics came to believe that one could only go to communion provided one had gone to confession. Thus in the old days the good Catholic went to confession on Saturday evening and to communion on Sunday morning. However, this practice developed out of a misunderstanding.*

The only time a Catholic has to confess to a priest is on the occasion of mortal sin. All other sinfulness is absolved ordinarily through communion. For the Easter duty then, it is only necessary to confess when one is in a state of mortal sin. Otherwise we are only obligated to receive communion, for after all communion is for sinners, not for saints. We are cele-

brating the truth that God loves us even though we are sinners. We do not have to get all cleaned up the night before and put on a false Sunday front in order to be acceptable at the Lord's table. In Jesus' time the respectable people criticized him for eating with sinners. Have his habits changed today?

The modern restoration of the liturgy makes the eucharist much more important in grass-roots Catholic life, for the liturgy becomes our school in Christianity. It acquaints us and our children with the basic stories of Jesus and it grounds us in the fundamental Christian vision or world outlook. Most of the material and experience communicated in pre-Vatican II Catholicism through the parochial school or through CCD is now communicated through the liturgy.

As we gather together each Sunday to celebrate the great deeds of God we journey again and again each year through the life of Jesus. Our year begins about the beginning of December with the season of Advent. During these four weeks we look forward to the consumation of Jesus' vision in his second coming, and with the prophets of the Old Testament we again look forward with Israel to his first coming. At Christmas we celebrate his entrance into our world—his birth.

Then in February or March we enter the great Christian penitential season of Lent. During this time each Christian examines his life to discover how he has failed to capture the vision of Jesus, and he seeks how he might be a better herald of Christian love. Lent prepares for the greatest Christian feast, Easter, when we celebrate Jesus' victory over sin and death. The Easter season lasts for fifty days, during which time we celebrate Jesus' ascension (forty days after Easter) when he was glorified by his Father. At the end of the Easter season (fifty days after Easter) we celebrate the feast of Pentecost as we remember how the Holy Spirit descended upon the disciples and the Church was born.

There are also certain other feasts of the Church on which Christians celebrate the eucharist together. These days include January 1 (one week after Christmas) when we celebrate Mary's motherhood. We also celebrate two other feast days of Mary. December 8 is the feast of her immaculate conception, when we remember how Mary through the power of God was preserved free from the snares of sin that entangle the rest of us, and August 15 celebrates Mary's assumption into the kingdom, an action which prefigures the eventual redemption of the world and the coming in glory and power of God's kingdom. Finally, on November 1 we celebrate and remember all those men and women who have succeeded in allowing the vision of Jesus to transform their lives. This is the feast of All Saints.

Christ's presence among us

Christians have often talked of the eucharist as a presence of Christ among his people. And his presence is very manifest in every celebration of the Mass. First, as Jesus promised, he is present whenever two or three are gathered together in his name. His Church is his very body. He is present also when his story and his message are proclaimed. The Scriptures are truly God's Word, somehow contained in our fragile words. When the message is proclaimed and heard among men, then Jesus, who is the Word of God, is present.

Christ is also present in the person of the priest or minister. The priest assumes the role that Christ performed at the Last Supper. He celebrates the eucharist in Christ's name. In the ritual action he ceases to be an individual. He now acts in the name of his Lord who is present to the community through this man. Just as God chose incredibly to become a man to reach men, so now he uses the person of the priest to be present to his people.

Then Christ is present in the bread and wine. Christians believe that in the mystery of this sacrament the bread and the wine truly become the body and blood of Jesus, given to men for their nourishment and salvation. He is present in the bread and wine without it seeming to be any less bread and wine than before. Throughout the centuries theologians have attempted to understand more profoundly this mystery and they have developed complex and elaborate theologies to aid in penetrating the mystery. But no matter how brilliant the insight, the mystery remains, and it remains at the center of Christian faith: our food and drink as long as we remain upon this earth. No Christian can explain it, but he firmly believes in Jesus' real presence in the eucharist. As Jesus was truly God without damage to his humanity, so in this sacrament he is truly present in his body and blood.

The eucharist is the source and nourishment for Christian experience. Its celebration makes people one in their communion with Christ. As the wheat scattered on the hillsides was made one in the bread, so we who are scattered over the earth are brought into one through the bread of Jesus broken so that all might be united in him and with one another.

In the eucharist we enter most closely into relationship with Christ as we hear his Word, partake of his body and blood, and join in union with our brothers to praise our Father. Strengthened by this communion we again go out into the world to bring men good news. We come together to renew and strengthen our faith so that we may continue our mission to the world. At the end of Mass the priest says, "The Mass is ended. Go forth to love and serve the Lord." To which every Christian replies: "Thanks be to God" both now and forever.

Important biblical texts concerning the eucharist are found in Mark 14:12-31, 1 Corinthians 11:17-34, and especially John 6.

 The Church Praying

Father, you are holy indeed,
and all creation rightly gives you praise.
All life, all holiness comes from you
through your Son, Jesus Christ our Lord,
by the power of the Holy Spirit.
From age to age you gather a people to yourself,
so that from east to west
a perfect offering may be made
to the glory of your name.

And so, Father, we bring you these gifts.
We ask you to make them holy by the power of your
    Spirit,
that they may become the body and blood
of your Son, our Lord Jesus Christ,
at whose command we celebrate this eucharist.
On the night he was betrayed,
he took bread and gave you thanks and praise.
He broke the bread, gave it to his disciples, and said:
Take this, all of you, and eat it:
this is my body which will be given up for you.
When the supper was ended, he took the cup.
Again he gave you thanks and praise,
gave the cup to his disciples, and said:
Take this, all of you, and drink from it:
this is the cup of my blood,
the blood of the new and everlasting covenant.
It will be shed for you and for all men
so that sins may be forgiven.
Do this in memory of me.

Let us proclaim the mystery of faith:
    Christ has died,
    Christ is risen,
    Christ will come again.

Father, calling to mind the death your Son endured
    for our salvation,
his glorious resurrection and ascension into heaven,
and ready to greet him when he comes again,
we offer you in thanksgiving this holy and living sac-
    rifice.

Look with favor on your Church's offering

and see the Victim whose death has reconciled us to
   yourself.
Grant that we, who are nourished by his body and
   blood,
may be filled with his Holy Spirit
and become one body, one spirit in Christ.
May he make us an everlasting gift to you
and enable us to share in the inheritance of your
   saints,
with Mary, the virgin Mother of God,
with the apostles, the martyrs, and all your saints,
on whose constant intercession we rely for help.

Lord, may this sacrifice which has made our peace
   with you
advance the peace and salvation of all the world.
Strengthen in faith and love your pilgrim Church on
   earth,
your servant Pope Paul, our bishop,
and all the bishops,
with the clergy and the entire people your Son has
   gained for you.
Father, hear the prayers of the family you have gathered here before you.
In mercy and love unite all your children,
wherever they may be.
Welcome into your kingdom our departed brothers
   and sisters,
and all who have left this world in your friendship.
We hope to enjoy forever the vision of your glory,
through Christ our Lord, from whom all good things
   come.

Through him,

with him,
in him,
in the unity of the Holy Spirit,
all glory and honor is yours,
almighty Father,
for ever and ever.
Amen.

(Eucharistic Prayer III)

The Christian Prays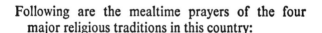

Following are the mealtime prayers of the four
   major religious traditions in this country:

Jewish:
Lift up your hands toward the sanctuary
   and bless the Lord.
Blessed are you, Lord our God, King of the universe,
   who bring forth bread from the earth.

Orthodox Christian:
Almighty and everlasting Father of us all,
we thank you for this food
   which strengthens and nourishes our bodies
   as your eternal Spirit sustains our souls,
and enables us to do good for others in your name
   and in the name of your Son, our Savior Jesus
   Christ.

Roman Catholic:
Bless us, O Lord, and these your gifts,
which we are about to receive from your bounty
through Christ our Lord. Amen.

Protestant:
Bless, O Lord, this food to our use,
and us to your service,
and make us ever mindful of the needs of others,
in Jesus' name. Amen.

Part IV
The Ethics of
Christianity

Introduction:

Conversion from

Maps to Tour Guides

*We Catholics had certainly mapped out the terri-
tory of the garden of Eden. We knew all the roads
and paths. We knew which roads to take where and
when. And we knew the blind alleys that did not lead
anywhere as well as the dangerous paths that led to
self-destruction and self-deceit. To be a Catholic
meant to know what was right and to act accordingly. Catholic moral theology was a clear, reasoned,
finely faceted jewel carved out of the notoriously difficult and obscure channels of human behavior.*

*We were not a people that could claim ignorance
of what to do in a given situation. In the past there
were plenty of road maps detailing our journeys
through the complex of everyday existence. Today,
however, maps appear to be in short supply. There
are no decent maps of this city of Jerusalem. It is
growing and changing too fast, and as soon as the
map is printed it is seen to be obsolete.*

*We long for the clear moral guidelines of our
youth. Today if we have a problem in moral behavior, the priest is often unable to give us clear guid-*

ance. He offers various alternative courses of behavior and says that we must consider the consequences of each choice. But the decision is now ours, and if we go back to Jesus' ethical teaching we do not receive much help there either. True, he does set out maxims for acceptable behavior in the kingdom, but often these admonitions seem impossible to follow. We cannot follow his teachings literally, for they demand too much of us. In the field of human behavior even more than in his teachings concerning God, Jesus is more a poet than a moralist. His new "laws" are meant to inspire us, not to enslave us. We will find no new road map here.

We needed a road map in the garden of Eden, we thought, so that we could get where we wanted to go —namely, heaven. But perhaps what we need in the city of Jerusalem is not a road map but a tour guide. Let us enjoy the sights of this city of God. Let us find out how we can become citizens in this city. As we become at home in the city, we will learn the names of the streets, but we will discover that we only use the streets in order to go places within the city, for there is always more than one way to get to a particular location in a city.

We do not need rules for ethical behavior so much as inspiration to create out of our life history something beautiful for God. We do not spend our time in the city walking the streets. We build houses, raise families and create out of our existence sparks of beauty that mirror the face of God.

10

The Wonder and
Mystery of Man

We have been talking about the Christian transformation of man in baptism and the eucharist. It is
now time to ask what man is. Is he basically good or
evil?

The human animal

What is man? He is an animal: the only one who
talks or thinks. He is a tool maker, a builder, a
painter. And in this he is unique. But he is also
unique as the animal who kills for the joy of killing.
He can at one time be higher than any other animal
and at another be more beastly and willingly cruel
than any other creature. He is the only animal who
laughs or smiles and the only animal who can destroy others merely by speaking.

He can improve himself or degrade himself. No
one would tell a dog to act like a dog—the animal
can do nothing else. But should a man act inappro-
priately, he will be told to act like a man. Man has
the freedom to become better, an angel, or worse, a

beast. He has the genius to build a hydrogen bomb and the depravity to explode one.

"Many awesome things there be under the sun, but none as awesome as man," says Sophocles. He is truly a marvel, the only creature who wonders. Only man knows of a world besides the external one: a world within himself as vast, deep and incomprehensible as the external universe of stars.

Man is torn between two poles: himself and others. Shall he escape the mob, be independent, go off on his own? Or should he join with others in building a society? Others impede his freedom and hurt him, but can he afford to cut himself off from their support, their companionship, their love?

Israel and social man

Israel found a response to the question of man at her very beginning. She was a society of free people. She was not a tyranny where all bow their will to the whim of the tyrant, but neither was she an anarchy where no man is his brother's keeper. Each person is part of the whole, each supports the society and in turn is supported.

Israel experienced God acting to build a human society. She learned to rely upon and even need the society of men. Man can only be man within a society: one man alone can not exist. God encounters Israel through society and history: he makes a covenant with a people, he establishes a nation, he sets up a monarchy to lead the nation, and when the society fails to live up to the covenant he sends individual prophets who give their lives to rescue the people and return them to God. God is revealed through politics, and the Israelite found his true identity as part of a people that God had chosen and created. Israel found the deepest meaning of her life as she relived year after year the Passover from slavery into freedom, and she shared that experience as a group of people with a common tradition.

Israel's story chronicles God's founding of a nation. But although we may desire to live together in society and want to dwell in peace, there is a disease which brings to nothing all our attempts: the disease of sin.

A hermit would not encounter sin. Assuming he could go about his life, scraping together a subsistence, eventually he would die of some natural cause or accident. But completely alone and never knowing another human being, he would live much as a cow —forging for food, his only care to escape destruction one day at a time, no thought because no language, his only emotions satisfaction or pain, his only hurts physical. He would exist and he would die and there would be an end of him.

But could such a being be a man? No. A man talks and thinks, remembers and laughs. But to do any of these things he must have fellows; therefore must get along with them and live in peace.

The blessing of law

It does not seem a very difficult thing to live in peace. All we need are a few rules, some conventions, a minimum of agreement and a little good will. On Mount Sinai God provided Israel with such a law. It guarded against division and strife arising within the society, offering ten simple rules designed to prevent sin. Honor your elders. Do not steal. Do not kill. Do not commit adultery. Do not bear false witness against your neighbor. Do not envy your neighbor. Worship the Lord as your only God. Do not worship false gods. Do not take the Lord's name lightly. Reserve one day a week to remember God.

There is nothing startling or unexpected in these ten commandments. Most of them form the basis for any cooperative living. Only the commands concerning God are unique to Israel. But there lies the secret to peace. Only under God can man be in harmony. When we place ourself in God's seat, society's fabric is stretched and torn. With no God, man in his pride becomes a god and arrogates to himself the privilege of abrogating the other commands. The proud man is above the law: he feels society should center around him.

Israel was taught that society can only work when it revolves not around man or a group of men but God. When God is not honored a false god is: the god of man's pride, the fateful cruel god of nature and her laws, the god of wealth and worldly success. Israel in her history followed all these gods, and because she did so she fell, crushed under her own sins.

The curse of law

But let us not stand on a peak and judge Israel. Let us take the commandments upon ourselves. They are quite simple and easy to understand. They are reasonable and no one would be unwilling to subscribe to them. Nor do they seem difficult to keep. With a little good will on the part of all we could make Israel's covenant a reality in our world.

But when we attempt to live seriously by these simple commands we begin to see the grave difficulty involved. They are broken constantly, and not only by the undesirable element of society. We break them continually ourselves. We may manage for a few days and congratulate ourselves. But what of the couple next door? You heard the quarrel they had last night until two in the morning, and you just have to tell someone about it. Or you become angry at your son because he left his tricycle in the drive again. Sure you had a right to become angry—but *that* angry? Because you had a rough day at work, does your little boy deserve the bile you have accumulated during the day? No one sets out to violate the society's bans on adultery. But before we know it we are seeing another man or woman, and we are hopelessly entangled in an affair. We now see the impossibility of conforming to the law of righteousness.

The harmonious society that the commandments were meant to produce never materializes. These ten guides toward good living given us by God come to be condemning judges of our behavior. Instead of leading us to happiness they accuse us of our failure. St. Paul goes so far as to say that they bring sin into the world because they hold up a mirror showing how far we have strayed from God and his ways. Before the law we lived in ignorance, but through the law we have seen the truth, and we cannot possibly live the truth. The more we try to succeed the greater our failure. The law provided for our improvement has only thrown into relief our meanness and wretchedness.

We know the good, we want to do the good, but we always fail to accomplish the good. We build a civilization, a perfect city, but there is a crack in the foundation. The worm eats away inside our noblest action and eventually brings it to nothing. We are doomed to failure. We build utopias and the very word tells us of our failure, for "u-topia" means "no-place." It cannot exist here in spite of its simplicity.

St. Paul knew acutely our dilemma which later theologians have called "original sin." Our imperfection accuses us and declares that we are not what we should be. Something has gone awry, and Paul lays the blame for this original sin upon man himself. For God is righteous and just—such is the two thousand year experience of Israel. The fault cannot be with him who detests evil and calls for its defeat. If not God, then we must acknowledge ourselves as somehow guilty. Nor is it an accidental defect: we are not automatons but free and responsible beings, and if we would live up to our responsibility then we must shoulder the sin, the disease, which has come to be part of being human.

Israel disobeyed the law and the law condemned her sin. How can man be reconciled, how can we be brought together with ourselves, our brothers and sisters and God? The law demonstrates our helplessness; we are left without hope of reconciliation and peace.

A faithful servant

What if one man in his life should be able to fulfill the law? We are inclined to say he would be a saint, a great leader of men. He would be admired, respected, even worshiped. But we must remember that he would have to live his life without sin in the depths of a world torn apart by sin. He would be a saint among sinners.

When we attempt to change ourselves, one of the first difficulties we encounter is our friends. The worst enemies of the man who gives up smoking are his smoking friends. They constantly remind him of cigarettes and unwittingly tempt him by smoking in his presence. Sometimes they even become indignant that he has stopped smoking because they see it as a judgment upon themselves.

How easy it would be to be sinless in a sinless society. But every time I attempt to live the law I am hurt by other men's sinfulness. The prophet Isaiah envisioned an Israel without sin, an Israel conforming to God. In a series of beautiful songs he told of such a faithful servant of God. He imagined Israel as an individual and the other nations as Israel's fellow men. The servant Israel led a blameless life. But because of her obedience and holiness she is hated by her fellows and put to death. She seems weak and ugly to look at; she is a laughingstock. The scorning nations spit upon her. Such is the lot of the sinless in a sinful world.

Healed by his stripes

Isaiah's songs of the sinless Israel were not fulfilled. However in Jesus the world found a sinless man—a man without blame, totally obedient to God. And the reward of such sinlessness was rejection by his fellow men. Our sin cannot stand holiness: something inside us relishes the downfall of a good man. Jesus' holiness was rewarded by a cross and death.

But in Jesus' life the old covenant had been lived and given flesh. Although not sinful, he had suffered death, the consequence of sin. But God refused to let sinful man prevail. Taking the "no" of Jesus' condemnation by man, he answered it with an eternal "yes" through the resurrection. Man had committed the most heinous sin possible: killing an innocent man. God responded by turning that crime into a victory and a triumph. The worst man could do was answered by the greatest God could do: Jesus conquered death and destroyed sin. He had lived a life free of sin and had merited eternal life with God. He had replaced Israel and had become God's true servant.

In Israel many men had represented one entity: in Jesus one man comes to represent all men. Through baptism into him we are made sinless and righteous. We do not deserve this favor, nor can we earn it. It is a gift of God. We stand in the right even though we have done the wrong. We are sinless even though we have sinned.

The power in Jesus' victory enables us to conquer sin in our own lives. We stand in his body and model ourselves upon him in the assurance that his victory is our victory and that in him we too can be sinless because we share his power over sin and death. The victory has already been accomplished in Jesus. All that remains is its realization in our own lives.

In Christ's body a new society is formed, freed from the bondage of sin and death. But although there is the power and the possibility of sanctity, there is also the acknowledgment that baptism does not entirely destroy the old man. If it did we would not be free: we would be determined toward holiness after baptism just as we were determined toward sin before. Sin still breaks out in the community of the saved, but it can never prevail—its death is already present.

The Church as Christ's body is sinless, but inasmuch as she is still in the world and composed of sinful men she is also sinful. She is the new Israel. The old Israel had a law which laid out the conditions for a peaceful and happy society. The new Israel has in the person of her Lord already fulfilled the law: peace and happiness are at hand. She needs to win no victory; she needs only make actual its results in her life. She is a bride in pilgrimage to her groom, and at the same time she is already there at his side.

The ten commandments are found in Deuteronomy 5.

The Song of the Suffering Servant is in Isaiah 52:13-53:12.

Paul speaks of Jesus and the law in Romans 5-7.

The Church Praying

Father,
we see your infinite power
in your loving plan of salvation.
You came to our rescue by your power as God,
but you wanted us to be saved by one like us.
Man refused your friendship,
but man himself was to restore it
through Jesus Christ our Lord.

Father in heaven,
the love of your Son led him to accept
the suffering of the cross
that his brothers and sisters might glory in new life.
Change our selfishness into self-giving.
Help us to embrace the world you have given us,
that we may transform the darkness of its pain
into the life and joy of Easter.

> (Ordinary Preface III and Opening Prayer
> for Fifth Sunday of Lent)

 **The Christian Prays**

To meet life one day at a time, one step at a time;
To have the strength and the will to keep on keeping
   on;
To have the wisdom to handle the affairs of my life;
To have the ability to make right and good decisions;
To have the courage to let the past go, to forge ahead
   resolutely;
To have the grace to meet each experience, ex-
   pectantly, happily;

To have the faith to know that there is no loss or
separation in God, that in him I am for ever with
those I love;

To have the vision to see the good in all things, the
Christ in all persons;

To have an awareness of God's presence, close, abiding;

To know that God will never fail me nor forsake me;

This is my prayer.

(Traditional)

11

The Christian's
Own Story

"Free at last"

Freedom from sin and death is the beginning of Christian life, not its end. In baptism man is made into Christ and has conquered. But how is he to live? What makes Christian existence different?

There is nothing very new in Christian ethics: no secret rule Christians follow unknown to other people. The difference is not in rules and law but in outlook and attitude.

Paul found that Jewish law only served to make man aware of his sin. This awareness would then lead to despair—for how could man possibly avoid sin and achieve peace with his fellows and God? The Christian knows that he too is sinful but that in spite of his sin he is freed from it through Jesus. Thus the Christian's life becomes an exploration of his new freedom, and with the power of the Holy Spirit he receives from Jesus in baptism and the eucharist he breaks the actual bondage of sin in his own life.

The Christian's life is a reflection upon and a variation of Jesus' story. He appropriates into his own life the freedom and power of Jesus over sin and death. And if this experience should become central, then his life will speak of the Jesus-experience to all he meets. The more he enters into Jesus' vision, the more his life will tell a story similar to that of Jesus.

The Christian makes real in his own life the love for God and for all people which Jesus had. He is able to forgive others when they wrong him; he becomes strong enough to return love for hate, right for wrong. He sees the necessity of love and realizes that love must be spent—it cannot be hoarded. So he makes service real in his life and gives love flesh.

Cross and glory

But if a Christian would live a Christ-life, can its reward be other than the cross? The world is still sinful and Christian life is bound to bring some form of suffering. Perhaps the cross takes the form of disease, or failure, or the loss of friends. Although he cannot escape sin and suffering, yet the Christian knows that suffering is not final; it cannot destroy him.

The cross is his victory: Christian suffering shows others the power of Jesus to transform and redeem man's sinful condition. Suffering, accepted in the faith that it cannot kill but has already met its defeat in the cross, tells the world a much different story than suffering given in to, despaired over and thought hopeless.

During the centuries Christians have made Jesus clearly visible in their lives. These men and women were truly other Christs, living Jesus' story in their own culture and age. And the Church has held these men and women up to other Christians for imitation. What does it mean to be a Christian? Consider Christ's saints.

A short glance at the infinite variety of saints convinces anyone of the freedom within the vision of Jesus. Francis of Assisi gave up everything—family, wealth, title—to follow Jesus as a pauper. Thomas More was chancellor of England under Henry VIII, yet he preferred to lose his position and finally his life rather than compromise his vision of Jesus. Isaac Jogues, a missionary to the American Indians, suffered cruel tortures at their hands willingly, hoping to bring them his vision of Jesus. Thomas Aquinas, Christ's scholar, at the time when the philosophy of Aristotle threatened Christian faith, brought the principles of Aristotelianism into the service of the faith. All for the greater glory of God!

Conscience's spur

Granted that every Christian should show forth Christ in his life, how can he achieve this goal in the concrete experiences of daily living? How can he decide whether one course of action is better than another?

The source of our decision-making process is that mysterious entity called a conscience. Whenever confronted with a major decision involving right and wrong, we supposedly follow this conscience. "Let your conscience be your guide." A Christian can do no better.

But what is a conscience? Is it always right? Two mothers of small children become pregnant again. One mother terminates her pregnancy while the other mother, although her family is big enough already, has her baby because she cannot in conscience have an abortion. Is each woman right? Is one conscience as good as another? Is what a man does indifferent so long as he thinks it is right? Hitler believed he was right and few would want to have seen him succeed.

Conscience is a person's sense of right and wrong. When confronted by a decision I do not decide on a mere whim. I have some idea whether a course of action is right or wrong, good or evil. I also wish to take account of my action's consequences.

Take a simple example: I am hungry and a basket of green apples lies before me. Should I eat them or not? A little boy might decide to eat them. But I as an adult would probably forego the pleasure. Foreseeing the stomach ache, I would consider it wrong to satisfy my hunger in this way. And the little boy, after he has suffered from the apples, would come to see the problem as I do: the immediate pleasure and good of eating the apples is not worth the misery and pain of the nausea.

This trivial example shows in part how conscience develops. It is not built into us—it grows and matures. Indeed most of our education consists in conscience development. It converts us from savages into civilized people; we do not kill each other over a slight misunderstanding, we do not cheat, we believe in respect, trust and fairness rather than chicanery, scheming and thievery, we do not eat green apples.

We are not born with an already-formed conscience, only with the capacity to develop one. The baby, cute as he is, is totally self-centered and demanding. But his education begins almost immediately: he must learn to control his urges to wet his diaper, he must learn to eat at certain times rather than when he happens to get hungry. He must learn the value of property—he cannot play with his mother's china. He must control his anger—he can not hit his sister every time he feels like it. And so it goes throughout his life.

We have many teachers: our parents most importantly, but also our culture: children in America soon learn that it is not good to get dirty, while mothers elsewhere may not be concerned about cleanliness at all. A child's peers greatly influence his conscience. When the child is old enough we put him into a school which teaches him how to get along in society. His mind is filled with the knowledge he will need to function in his society, and his behavior is changed and modified so that he will fit into society.

Finally, religion plays an important role: we are taught that some things are good and others evil because God has said so. If a child wishes to act in the face of the disapproval of his parents, his friends, his teachers and God himself, he weighs the situation and probably decides that although it would be very gratifying to belt his sister in the mouth, it would also produce some very ungratifying side-effects far outweighing the initial pleasure.

Considering again the two pregnant mothers we see that there are many variations of conscience possible within a society, and of course there are many differences between various societies. Two people may not assimilate the culture's taboos against certain behavior to the same extent. Or they may emerge with different consciences because of a difference in their parents' outlook or their religious affiliation. When the conscience-building process fails, another variation, the criminal or deviate, results.

Is there any element of this fluid conscience that rises above happenstance? Is our conscience simply an accident decreed by upbringing, environment and genes? Are we ultimately slaves to this censor in our brain?

The God of conscience

Israel found that conscience need not be an arbitrary whim fate plays upon us. It should be directed by something larger than ourselves, our parents, or our society. The source and molder of conscience should be God, for only he can reveal to us the truth. Israel read her history as a slow education of her conscience by God. She believed there was progress: while once it was acceptable to wipe out an enemy down to the last woman and child, Israel later realized that such an action was not really consonant with the reality God had revealed to her.

God's law showed a path between the anarchy of relativism where every man is his own law and the suffocation of tyranny where one man decides the law for all. God's law was a freeing experience because it provided the structures within which a society could live in peace and harmony.

But Israel's law too became a tyranny. Unable to hold to its spirit, she degraded its observance into a formalism: she obeyed the letter and thought that sufficient. Law became an end rather than a means.

Troubler of the complacent

Jesus is no destroyer of Israel's law. True, he replaces it, but he did so not by abolition but by fulfillment. Men too easily gloat in self-satisfaction. If I have managed to keep the Sabbath holy, if I have paid my respects to God, if I have not cheated on my neighbor, then I can sit down with a certain satisfaction. I have fulfilled my duty. God is duly appeased.

"If you should think evil against a man in your mind, then you have as well as killed him in the flesh." These words shake us out of our complacency. *God* is the fulfillment of the law. Law is not an end in itself; it is a beginning.

Israel's conscience had become static. It was formed and then simply referred to in determining how to act. Make the law your conscience, then regulate your actions accordingly. How many of us still think this way? We know right from wrong; we are constructive, law-abiding members of society; our faults are minor and forgivable.

Jesus refused to accept this complacence. The holiness of God goes far beyond the minimalism of the law. He accused the Israelites of a dead conscience. As long as we live we must strive toward God and his holiness. Our call is not to the security *and* the tyranny of a static conscience. We must expand our vision and be free of all tyranny.

Conscience may be wrong; it will always be imperfect. In Jesus we have a model and a vision of God which cannot be minimalized. We need no law because in him we are already just. But we do have his call to go continually beyond ourselves. And his teachings serve as guideposts along our way. Love one another as you love yourself. Return love for hatred. Let forgiveness replace vengeance. Be guided by charity rather than justice. These are not laws but models which found their perfect expression in Jesus' life.

A Christian is free from the tyranny of conscience. The law had said: Do this and live. Jesus says: Live and do this. We are not justified by our conscience; we are justified by God. Nor are we tied to our conscience: often it should be corrected through a deeper understanding of Jesus.

Conscience continues to be formed every day of our life—through God's Word in Holy Scripture, through the teachings of the Christian community, through encyclicals (official teachings of the pope in the name of the entire Church), through our family and friends, and, most important through prayer.

We cannot abdicate our freedom—we must follow God's voice in our conscience, even it it be against the advice of parents, country, friends or pope. If we do violate our conscience we run the risk of stifling the Holy Spirit who dwells within us, for our God does not now primarily reside in a book, or in a law, but in a people of whom I am part. I may be wrong in a certain matter, but I also know that the Spirit dwells in me and can speak through me. If we are open to advice and change, if we are sincere in seeking God's will, then we can only follow God; anything else is tyranny and slavery. He is our only judge and corrector; we are under no law and will be judged only by God's mercy seen in Jesus Christ.

Many Catholics have also fallen into the trap of law. After all, law is comforting when it regulates your life. It takes the guesswork and uncertainty out. If we could just accept the law we would find that life makes fewer demands upon us. And it seemed at times that in the old Church there was a law for every situation, but actually the Church made laws only when she had to. A law merely insures a minimal commitment to Christ's vision. It is not a law that to be a good Christian one need only attend the eucharist once a week. It is the law that to be any kind of Catholic at all one must attend eucharist once a week. It is not the law that to be a good husband one must not commit adultery. It is the law that to be any kind of husband at all—even the most rotten one—one must not commit adultery. If I commit adultery, I am not merely a bad spouse; I have destroyed the marital relationship altogether.

If we as Catholics are content to let the Church's law regulate our life, we are missing the true meaning of that law. The law only acts to set minimum standards for inclusion in the Christian community. The Christian acts not from the law. Rather we are drawn toward the kingdom by the vision of Christ. Our life and actions are inspired by the power of the Holy Spirit which dwells within us and draws us home to the Father.

Christian behavior is not following rules. Christians are not a people of the law. They cannot go through life following the laws and keeping their noses clean. If we are made righteous because we stand in Jesus, if we are sons and daughters of God because he was God's Son, then our life must model his. As sons and daughters, Christians are responsible for their brothers and sisters. We are not called to obey some law but to freely give ourselves to our fellow man. We are called to show our freedom in action.

Mercy tempers justice in our lives. If a brother in need asks for money, it is justice to give him what he needs and it is mercy to give him more. It is justice to see that no man suffers because of his color; it is love and mercy to welcome him as a brother. It is justice to repay a wrong with punishment; it is mercy to forgive. If we would stand in Jesus, then we must act like Jesus: love knows no limit.

"Sleepers, awake!"

One of the earliest Christian hymns had a phrase concerning "sleepers who wake from the dark." Christians are people who have awakened from the sleep of inaction and indifference. In Jesus we see what it means to be truly alive. Life is only alive when it is motivated by love. Selfishness is another word for death. Life means other people and it means living for others.

We wake up to the needs of our fellow men: first their physical needs of clothing, health and food, then their needs of education, cultural enrichment and spiritual happiness. We meet these needs because we are thankful: our need for meaning has been met in Jesus Christ. And the only adequate response we can make consists in sharing our joy with others.

We wake to the needs of our country. We teach, we heal, we become a public servant. Of course not all can act in such a capacity. But all citizens share the responsibility to bring about conditions of peace and harmony. As Christians we awake from our lethargy. We take our citizenship seriously. We exercise our right to vote with intelligence. We participate in the formation of public policy. We voice our opinion on issues.

We wake to the needs of mankind. World peace remains a mere dream unless we dedicate ourselves to concrete action. We cannot shrug off responsibility if we would be alive. The fight against disease requires our aid, through political action, or through economic support of various agencies, or through a scientific career.

We wake to the needs of the Christian community. We may educate children in the faith, visit sick members of the community, or help in a soup kitchen which feeds derelicts. We can help financially to support the Church's mission of good news. We could devote our lives to some form of Christian ministry. We can offer our talents to help in the celebration of the liturgy.

These are only a very few of the possible extensions of Christ's vision and action into the world. No one can hope to do more than a little. Some are called to do more, some less. But we all have a freedom to choose to live our life, not to let our life live us. Our life is free, a gift, not dictated by fate or chance. We are commissioned to make of our life a story, a song: a story that speaks of what we believe in, a song of life's meaning, of a purpose to living. If our story does not betray our vision, then Jesus is made flesh once more on this earth: another particle of creation is lifted up into God and made divine.

> The most famous passage of Jesus' teaching is the Sermon on the Mount in Matthew 5—7.
>
> Paul explains to the Romans how a Christian should act in Romans 12—15:13.
>
> John places in Jesus' mouth one of the most beautiful prayers for the care of his followers in John 17.

The Church Praying

Priest: My brothers and sisters, to prepare ourselves
to celebrate the sacred mysteries, let us call to mind our sins.

All: I confess to almighty God,
and to you, my brothers and sisters,
that I have sinned through my own fault
in my thoughts and in my words,
in what I have done,
and what I have failed to do;
and I ask blessed Mary, ever virgin,
all the angels and saints,
and you, my brothers and sisters,
to pray for me to the Lord, our God.

Priest: May almighty God have mercy on us,
forgive us our sins,

and bring us to everlasting life.

All: Amen.

(Rite of Penance during Eucharist)

The Christian Prays

A Christian Examination of Conscience

What follows is an attempt to provide a guideline for assessing our lives as Christians. These guidelines set very high standards. No one can possibly meet them all. We all fall seriously short of the model of Jesus. But as Christians we also realize that we can afford to have such high ideals because we will not be condemned for failure to achieve them. We are loved in spite of our failings. This love of God gives us the courage and the incentive to try ever anew.

We can be sure that we are in God only when we are living the same kind of life as Christ lived (1 John 2:5).

A young man once asked Jesus, "Master, what must I do?" And Jesus replied, "What does the law say?" The youth answered, "You must love the Lord your God with all your heart, soul, strength and mind, and your neighbor as yourself." "Do this," said Jesus (Luke 10:25-28).

A Christian deepens his love of God:

- through a life nourished by deep and inner prayer which feeds on the prayer life of the Church herself.
- through frequent meditation on God's Word in Scripture.

- through participation in Christ's sacraments where the Christian enters more deeply into the vision of Jesus.
- by celebrating each Sunday as the day of the Lord and joining with fellow Christians in the eucharist on that day and on other important feast days.
- through a spirit of sacrifice and self-denial by which we learn to become more concerned for others and less self-centered.

Christian love for the neighbor means:

- I can exclude no one from universal brotherly love.
- I will live more for others than for myself.
- I am faithful to my friends and dependable.
- I am not haughty or cynical toward others.
- I try to live in a spirit of genuine honesty and truth.
- I do not restrict my love by barriers of race, social class or creed.
- I express my love especially in my service and generosity to the poor and the powerless.
- I try genuinely to listen to others.
- I am considerate of others and their property.
- my words and judgments are made in a spirit of kindness and charity.
- I easily pardon the weaknesses and sins of others against me.
- I am prompt to ask forgiveness when I have hurt or sinned against others.
- I go out of my way to help my neighbor.

● I am concerned for the effect of my actions and words upon others.

When Christ freed us, he meant us to remain free. Therefore stand your ground, and do not submit again to a yoke of slavery (Gal. 5:1).

A Christian is free:

● from slavery to his instincts; whatever the Christian does, he does as a free agent.
● from idols such as money, material comfort, power, luxury, and false forms of love.
● from the sin of self-love and egotism.
● from prejudice which narrows love and makes it unlike the love of God.
● from the need to defend and justify oneself constantly. He can admit his sins and failures, and he willingly accepts helpful criticism and advice.
● from falsehoods in his search for truth. He does not accept imposed answers, nor does he restrict himself to the opinions of any one "class," whether it be a social class or a peer group.

My dear people, let us love one another, for love comes from God and everyone who loves is of God (1 John 4:7).

God's love is made visible in the sacrament of marriage. Therefore the Christian:

● exhibits a healthy attitude toward sex as a gift of God and avoids the extremes of pru-

dishness and licentiousness.
- avoids all love of the flesh for its own sake.
- accepts the vocation to marriage or to celibacy as a gift of God and finds in his particular vocation a means of drawing closer to God's love.
- is totally faithful to his spouse as a reflection of God's fidelity to his people.

Christian love radiates outward into the family. The Christian:

- honors his parents and shows them respect.
- is not ashamed of his parents or relatives because of some involuntary fault such as modest origins or foreign accent.
- is willing, when able, to return his parents' love by providing for them in old age and through other acts of tenderness and loving concern.
- is concerned to provide in his life a good example for his children to imitate.
- provides for his children through emotional, economic and educational security.

Go into the entire world and proclaim the good news to all creation (Mark 16:16).

Every Christian has a mission to his fellow men. Therefore:

- he supports the Church's work through his talents and money.
- he is not ashamed to reveal himself as a

Christian and to give witness to his belief.

- he gives money and time to working for different charitable causes.
- he takes his political responsibilities seriously.
- he keeps informed on current events and votes intelligently.

The Christian is mindful that he has been appointed the guardian over God's creation.
Therefore:

- he uses his environment without polluting it unnecessarily.
- he is careful in his use of material goods and avoids carelessness and excessive waste.

The Christian recognizes his occupation as an excellent means to express his love of God.
Therefore:

- he does his job without laziness or carelessness.
- he is careful to acquire and maintain occupational and technical competence.

Father, may they be one in us, as you are in me and I in you (John 17:21).

The Christian is called to make visible in the world the unity already present in God. Therefore:

- he strives to overcome dissension and misunderstandings and to create in their place a spirit of peace and brotherhood.

- he begins the work of peace in his own life, in his work and in his family; then through his money and talents he extends that peace throughout the world.
- he opposes war vigorously and will only allow himself to fight in self-defense and when peaceful measures have been exhausted.
- he is eager through prayer and work to help heal the sinful divisions that hurt the unity of Christ's Church.

There is a variety of gifts but always the same Spirit: there are varieties of service, but all are for the same Lord (1 Cor. 12:4).

The Christian serves God by:

- letting the entire community benefit from his gifts and capabilities.
- developing to their fullest his own innate talents, cultivating his mind, and keeping his body healthy.
- using his talents in a spirit of humility and service, without either pride or boasting.
- refusing to limit his service to any specific group, be it parish, family or friends.
- showing respect and appreciation for the talents and gifts of others.
- being willing to work with and cooperate with others in group projects.
- avoiding an attitude of domination when in a position of authority or an attitude of rebelliousness when working under another.

Brothers and sisters, you will always have trials, but when they come, treat them as a happy privilege— your faith is only put to the test to make you patient (James 1:2).

The Christian:

- is patient with his own faults and those of others.
- never despairs since he knows that God's goodness and mercy will triumph and that he is loved by God in spite of his sins.
- bears hardship and suffering ungrudgingly, mindful of Jesus' suffering.

"Lord, be merciful to me, a sinner!"

"Your sins are forgiven. Now go, my brother, and sin no more."

God deliver us from sullen saints.

(St. Theresa of Avila)

Part V

The Rituals of

Christianity

(continued)

12

Sacraments of Healing —

Reconciliation and Anointing

The symbolics of healing

Sacraments are not magic. They do not overwhelm with their power. And most Christians unfortunately often fail to live up to their call. The Church is holy and at the same time sinful—she is composed of people who have been given Christ's vision, baptized into his name and fed on his body, but yet allow strife, anger, envy, lust, and malice to dominate their life at times. When strife and sin appear in a human community, that society is hurt. If one member of a family injures another, the family suffers. If the injury is severe the family is torn, perhaps destroyed—divorce looms on the horizon. Similarly, a serious sin alienates a man from his fellow men: his relationships with others in that society are threatened or even terminated. He finds himself cut off—exiled from the group.

Jesus brought reconciliation. He calls us to come together and forgive each other. The family of man torn by wars, feuds, bitterness, harsh words and greed must be reunited in a fellowship of forgiveness and reconciliation. Jesus' ministry is one of healing.

Healing is a universal phenomenon manifested under two symbols. The first is associated with physical healing. Oil was often used as a salve applied to wounds to promote their healing. Even today we recognize certain medicinal properties in oil. It soothes the pain of burns; it can be used to clean a person; it restores health and vitality to dried skin and gives the person a youthful look.

The second symbol of healing lifts us out of the animate world into purely human experience. We have seen symbols so far as material parts of our earth: water, fire, oil, bread and wine. But forgiveness is a particularly human symbol of healing: it is not an artifact; we cannot place it before us on a table and inspect it. We want to say that it is spiritual rather than material.

But forgiveness has a very definite material aspect. For as a human reality it is as much a part of our bodily self as of some spiritual self. Forgiveness occurs after a split has taken place between people. Something has been done to upset or even destroy a relationship. A husband has let his anger flare out against his wife; good friends let envy for one another eat away at their friendship. When a relation is broken, if the breach is to be healed it must be done through the symbol of forgiveness.

And forgiveness always involves some bodily action, even if no more than saying the words, "I'm sorry," and hearing in response, "It's all right." Depending upon the culture and the people, forgiveness takes on almost an infinite variety of bodily forms all relating to the request of forgiveness and the granting of pardon. A husband brings home a bouquet of roses and his wife replies by a warm kiss.

A child goes out of his way to do some chore, and the mother in turn offers a cookie as a token of her forgiveness.

No matter the form, forgiveness always involves something material, a word, a formula, an embrace, a tear. It also involves a personal interaction. The offender confesses he is wrong and asks for forgiveness. The wronged party accepts the request and forgives. The people are reconciled and the relationship restored.

Inconstant Isreal

Inasmuch as Israel was a nation held together under the leadership of God, every sin and disruption of a man's relations with his neighbor threatened the fabric of Israel's society, and therefore man's relation to God. Every sin against one's neighbor was a sin against God inasmuch as God communicates to man through the nation and within the national and societal structures of Israel. There is no sin solely against God—all sin is social, against one's fellow man.

Israel's prophetic teaching was of a just God. God is righteous, holy, and abhors sin. In the eyes of Israel's prophets, Israel fell to the sword of her enemies because she refused to live in holiness and righteousness. Brother slew brother; man cheated and robbed his fellows; truthfulness was held of little value. The society degenerated; it became rotten and ripe for the conquest. God, being righteous, gave his people over to their just deserts.

But if God is just, he is also merciful, and the theme of his mercy appears also in the prophets. He will bring down judgment upon Israel, but only so that she might come to her senses and return to him. She must return to the covenant God had made with her in which he showed how people must live together in peace and harmony. He is willing to forgive if only Israel will repent and ask forgiveness. And in the future the prophets see Israel re-established with a new covenant—a covenant written in men's hearts. The righteousness of God shall overcome and heal the divisiveness of man. As the prophet Isaiah saw, "Nation shall not lift sword against nation nor be trained for war."

The blind see, the lame walk!

That new day has come in the person of Jesus. An important part of Jesus' ministry was healing. He made the blind see, the lame walk—and this was one of the signs of the great day Isaiah and the prophets had foretold. He healed men's bodies and their spirits. A lame man was once brought to him to be cured. Jesus said to the man, "Your sins are forgiven." Immediately the scribes and Pharisees, men educated in the Jewish faith, were horrified. Any Jew knew that only God could forgive sins. Then Jesus turns to them and asks which is more difficult, to heal a lame man or to forgive sins. The theologically correct answer of course was the latter, but the old maxim says seeing is believing. "So that you may believe I have power to forgive men's sins I say to this man, get up and walk: your sins are forgiven."

And the lame man walked, the Gospel reports.

The forgiveness of sins and the healing of man's physical infirmities were two important aspects of Jesus' ministry. So that his Church could carry on that ministry in his name, Jesus imparted to his disciples the power to heal spiritually and physically. The Acts of the Apostles depicts Peter and the other apostles carrying on this healing ministry.

At first the disciples understood this power to forgive sins primarily in terms of baptism. This sacrament washes a man clean from any sins he may have committed. And early Christianity demanded an exemplary moral and holy life from its converts. If a Christian fell into serious sin such as adultery, he was expelled from the Christian community.

In the first centuries four sins were thought worthy of excommunication (expulsion from the Church): murder, adultery, heresy (holding a theology that had been declared false) and apostasy (deserting or refusing to testify in public that one was a Christian). People were cut off from the Church for such acts and it was questionable whether they could ever be readmitted. Eventually the Church decided that such sinners could be restored to union provided that they repented and did penance.

Around the eighth century Christians began seeking out monks (men who had retired from worldly life for a life of Christian perfection) for spiritual guidance. They confessed their faults to these monks and received pardon and a penance to perform. This custom grew into the present sacrament of reconciliation.

While the Church has not always practiced this sacrament as modern Catholics are familiar with it, she has always been aware that Jesus has put into her hands the power to forgive sins in his name. This assurance has remained constant, but how the Church has employed this power throughout the ages has changed considerably.

Be reconciled and healed!

In recent years our practice of penance has again undergone considerable change. Indeed its importance and even its very existence in our life may have been called into question. When we were young we were pretty much taught that confession was a preparation for communion. Indeed many Catholics felt that it was not possible to receive communion unless one had first gone to confession. The old interpretation of the Easter duty as including both confession and communion did much to aid this misunderstanding. Today there are probably few Catholics who feel entirely satisfied with the place of confession in their lives.

Some are unable to deal with confession at all. They have too many bad memories of the box. Perhaps for this reason they fail to receive communion except during Easter time when they drag themselves through confession. Or they may have even left the Church rather than continue being what they consider an unworthy Catholic. Or perhaps they have rejected confession as one of the "things thrown out in the change." They live good lives and probably receive communion every week or even more often, but the sacrament of reconciliation forms no part of the Christian life.

None of the above Catholics has a healthy attitude toward the sacrament of reconciliation. And fortunately today with just a little re-education we can change our attitudes toward this sacrament, and in the process enrich our vision of Jesus. Let us begin by considering the appropriate times for the celebration of this sacrament.

The only time that a Catholic absolutely must go to private confession to a priest is when he is in the state of mortal sin. We all remember the catechism definitions of mortal sin. However in spite of the book learning we usually managed to inculcate the attitude that almost anything could be a mortal sin. If we wished to be good Catholics, after almost every peccadillo we went scurrying to the confessional. Mortal sin was the bogey man behind every locked door, every temptation. However, as adults we should no longer fear the bogey man, and we should also be able to dispel our fears of mortal sin in the light of reasonable day. A mortal sin is a serious offense of whose gravity we must be fully aware when we commit it, and we must commit this sin freely and without coercion. Using this definition, not many of us are presently guilty of mortal sin. When we have committed a mortal sin with full knowledge and freely, we will know it; there will be no doubt in our mind.

But to say that we are not in mortal sin certainly does not mean that we are not sinful. We are more shot full of sin than Swiss cheese has holes. The old Church preferred to call this venial sin, and venial sin was not held to cut us off from God as mortal sin does.

*No, venial sin does not cut us off from our fellow
man and from God, but it certainly does put obsta-
cles in the way of God's kingdom. With friends like
us God doesn't need enemies. Sin is sin, and it has
no part in the kingdom. It is our sinfulness—our selfishness, our lack of forgiveness, our hatreds, our
prejudices, our laziness—which prevents the kingdom from being established in our day. Too often in
the past we Catholics directed all our attention to
mortal sin: this was the serious sin. And it is serious
sin—it cuts us off from communication with both
other people and God. We regarded other sin as insignificant, yet it is that ordinary, petty, stupid sinfulness fermenting. within us that turns the milk of
the kingdom into bad cheese and makes the honey
rancid.*

*Our failure to celebrate the sacrament of confes-
sion as frequently in our lives today as was the case
in our past is not necessarily a degeneration of our
faith, for our idea of mortal sin and its frequency is
much different today. However, if our diminishing
practice of confession goes along with a failure to acknowledge our sinfulness, then we are losing a vital
element of Jesus' vision. Modern Catholics are
sometimes so overwhelmed by the rediscovery of the
joy in Jesus' message as well as their liberation from
many of the false conceptions in the old Church that
they take an overly optimistic view of man and the
world.*

*We think in our almost new-found faith that the
kingdom is at hand, but such an attitude will quickly
lead to disappointment and even despair, for we are
still sinners, and that sad fact is as much a part of*

Jesus' vision as the fact that we are children of God. If our sinfulness fails to play an important part in our religion, our religion will fail to provide meaning in our life when things go wrong—when we hurt others or are hurt in turn.

The primary way in which we acknowledge our sinfulness and celebrate our forgiveness by God is the eucharist. In the past we have tended to stress the eucharist either as the making present of Jesus' sacrifice or as the reception of holy communion. However, our focus upon these two aspects has neglected other dynamics which are also operating. One of the most important of these other dimensions is that of confession and reconciliation. In fact, we could say that the eucharist is the ordinary way in which our sinfulness is forgiven by God.

Thus the actual sacrament of reconciliation is the extraordinary manner of celebrating forgiveness. As was said before, the only time as Catholics that we have to confess directly to a priest is when a mortal sin has been committed. And even then, if it is not possible to make a confession, we can still be forgiven by God. Confession is a sure sign-symbol of God's forgiveness, but it is not the only way in which God may forgive and reconcile us. Confession to a priest is necessary in the case of mortal sin because it not only restores us to communion with God, but it also restores us to communion with our fellow Christians from whom we had been cut off by sin.

Furthermore we may celebrate the sacrament of reconciliation in a number of ways today. As an individual we may choose to celebrate the sacrament as in the old days with the aid of the confessional, but we may also receive the sacrament in the priest's study or any other suitable place. This change of place, as well as the fact that we may now celebrate the sacrament face to face, makes for a more relaxed and personal experience as opposed to the anonymity of the confessional.

As far as the content of our confession is concerned there is no need (and little benefit) to limiting it to the formulas of our childhood. True, we were taught that we had to confess all of our sins as well as the number of times we committed them, but this rule is only applicable to mortal sins. (It makes some difference whether we have murdered one or five people, but not much difference whether we blew up at our kids three or five times this week.) For ordinary sinfulness it is not so essential, and the Church does not require the grimy details.

We should consider the act of confession ordinarily as a spiritual inventory or, better, as a mini-retreat. Decide to devote a whole afternoon or at least a couple of hours to a consideration of your life. Where are you going? What are your ideals? How are you living up to those ideals? What are your relationships with others like? Do you often find yourself jealous? Impatient? Domineering?

When you have concluded your examination, go to the priest and talk over your situation. Together perhaps you can discover ways in which the vision of Jesus may shine more brightly in your life.

In the past we thought of confession primarily in terms of listing our sins, receiving a penance, and then obtaining absolution. Our overwhelming image of the experience was judgmental. We probably even find it strange to talk about "celebrating" the sacrament of confession, and yet the true Christian experience regards this action as a celebration. When Augustine wrote his Confessions, *it was not so much to tell all his sins as to praise the mercy and the love of God for him in spite of the fact that he was a sinner. Similarly (outside of mortal sin) we approach confession not so much to reveal our sins (God knows we are sinful) but to celebrate in our lives the wonderful forgiveness and reconciliation of the Holy Spirit.*

Catholics today are also rediscovering the community dimensions of reconciliation. It cannot be emphasized enough that a Christian is first of all a member of a family, a society, a nation. Sin cuts him off from God *because* it has destroyed his relation to his neighbor. Reconciliation restores the sinner's relation to his fellow Christians at the same time that it restores him to unity with God.

Catholicism emphasizes the need to confess one's sins to a priest so greatly not because man cannot confess directly to God: he can and does. But his relation to God is as part of a people. God has become man and taken on a human body; he has chosen to work through human realities and human structures. He has become visible first in Jesus and today in our brothers, particularly our brother Christians. And he offers us reconciliation through men, representatives of his Church. Sin cuts us from the Church as much as from God. The sacrament of reconciliation through the person of the priest, representing the Church, receives the sinner back into communion.

This communal aspect of reconciliation is emphasized through special reconciliation services. Here Christians come together to pray, meditate and examine their lives. How have they been living up to the light they carry within them? Have they treated their brother as a brother? At a point within this service there is the opportunity to go to a priest and confess privately. Then the priests give absolution to the people together. Thus the community is healed, brought back together and washed clean again.

There is no absolute rule on the place of the sacrament of reconciliation in a Christian's life. It is necessary if he has sinned gravely: if he has destroyed or seriously wounded his relations with another person. Hopefully such a serious sin will be an infrequent occurrence. But if we do not often fall into serious sin, we do fail to live up to our calling. Much of our life has not yet been transformed into Christ, and the sacrament of reconciliation used in a mature manner becomes a gifted moment when we can review our actions and thoughts in the light of the commission we received in confirmation. Acknowledging those areas in need of improvement, we receive Christ's healing power enabling us to continue to grow into his being. Reconciliation is the most personal of the sacraments: a meeting with the Lord who heals and reconciles. Too often in the past Catholics have thought of this sacrament in terms of being judged; its real value lies in hope and forgiveness.

> Psalm 51 is one of Israel's great songs of lament for her sins.
>
> John 11 recounts Jesus' raising of Lazarus from the dead and shows his power over life.

Jesus passes on his authority to forgive
sins to his disciples in John 20:19-29.

 **The Church Praying**

There are now officially three ways in which Catholics may celebrate the sacrament of reconciliation. When we celebrate the sacrament in a service with several other people, there may be an opportunity for individual confession of sins to a priest, or in certain circumstances there may be a general confession of sins (the people acknowledge their sinfulness but do not confess individually to a priest) followed by general absolution. The third form which reconciliation may take is the rite of individual reconciliation, and it is this form that we shall explain now.

To prepare for the sacrament, take some time alone and in quiet to examine your life. Make use of the examination of conscience in the preceding chapter, and then go to the priest either in the confessional or in a room set aside for the sacrament at your church.

When you enter, the priest will welcome you. You may then begin by making the sign of the cross, saying:

In the name of the Father, and of the Son, and of the Holy Spirit. Amen.

Then the priest will invite you to have trust in God, in these or similar words:

May God, who has enlightened every heart,
help you to know your sins
and trust in his mercy.

You should respond:

Amen.

Then the priest might read a text of Scripture which proclaims God's mercy and calls us to conversion.

At this point you may confess your sins. Begin by mentioning the length of time since your last confession. If you have since that time committed any serious sins, mention them along with the number of times they were committed. Then mention anything else on your mind. You might talk about attitudes toward your family, your faith, and your work. Mention any difficulties you have been having lately, and, if you wish, ask for advice in certain areas. If you have trouble making the confession, simply ask the priest to help you. When you have finished your confession, you might say:

For these and for all the other sins in my life I ask forgiveness.

The priest will then speak to you of those matters about which you have asked for advice, and he will also give you a penance to do which will help you make restitution for your sins and help you change your way of life. Then he will ask you to express your sorrow for your sins, which you may do in these or similar words:

Remember, Lord, your compassion and mercy you showed long ago.

Do not recall the sins and failings of my youth.

In your mercy remember me, Lord, because of your goodness.

Then the priest extends his hands over your head and says:

God, the Father of mercies,
through the death and resurrection of his Son
has reconciled the world to himself
and sent the Holy Spirit among us

for the forgiveness of sins;
through the ministry of the Church
may God give you pardon and peace;
and I absolve you from your sins
in the name of the Father, and of the Son,
and of the Holy Spirit.

You respond: **Amen.**

The priest continues: **Give thanks to the Lord, for he is good.**

You respond: **His mercy endures forever.**

Then the priest dismisses you, saying words such as:

Go in peace,
and proclaim to the world
the wonderful works of God,
who has brought you salvation.

The Christian Prays

We fall, O God,
and can go no farther.
We are paralyzed
and cannot stand again.
Sustained by the faith of your Church
we come to you,
for who can forgive sins
but you alone?
Heal us and raise us up
for the sake of your mercy
and of Jesus our brother.
Did you not raise him from the dead?
He lives with you
for this world and for all ages.

(Huub Oosterhuis, **Your Word Is Near**)

**The lame walk, the blind see,
and the poor hear the good news!**

The healing of physical maladies formed a prominent dimension of Jesus' ministry. These healings
were usually classified as miracles, but we have seen
that they were meant to be signs that the kingdom of
God was in some sense present in Jesus. The Church
too is a sign of God's kingdom, and as a sign of that
kingdom she shares in the ministry of healing. The
professions of medicine and nursing have always
been considered ministries by the Church. Indeed the
Church is largely responsible for the development of
hospitals and other institutions that care for the sick.
She considers the ministry of healing to be so important a sign of the kingdom that many of the mis-
sionaries carrying the good news of Jesus to poorer
nations were themselves also trained as doctors and
nurses.

This ministry of healing forms a prominent element of the Church's sacramental ministry. Whenever a Christian is seriously ill, a priest should be
called to administer the sacrament of the anointing
of the sick. The priest comes to the sick person and
together with the family prays for a restoration of
health. Then he anoints the person with holy oil in
Christ's name. Oil has always been looked upon by
men as having medicinal properties, and it is this
meaning of healing that is communicated in the action of anointing.

This sacrament sanctifies or makes holy the Christian's illness. We tend to think of illness as evil; it is
something to be shunned. There is no good in it. Naturally the Christian does not seek sickness, but on

the other hand we do not see sickness and suffering as only evil and useless. Sickness often offers us opportunities to re-evaluate our lives and to reorder our priorities. Often in sickness we are able to see and appreciate meaning in the vision of Jesus that we had not seen in health. The sacrament of anointing reveals to the Christian a special openness to God which illness often makes evident.

However, this sacrament not only reminds the Christian of Jesus' vision in time of suffering, but it also provides a means for the entire Christian community to join in prayers for the sick person. Today it is permissible to celebrate the sacrament of anointing in church in the context of the eucharist. There the community can pray for its sick and elderly and ask that the Lord will be with them in their suffering and their fears. These people are often shunned and ignored in our society today. Yet often through their sickness they have achieved a better appreciation and understanding of the vision of Jesus than we healthy people enjoy. They have much to share with us, and they can only do that if we include them as part of our living community.

We Christians also believe that this sacrament possesses power to heal the person. We are not talking about magic. Sacraments do not replace medicine, and the sick person does not infallibly recover, but faith does have healing power. The spirit does have power over the flesh. Through sickness and weakness the Christian might come close to understanding the meaning of Jesus. Thus the power of the Holy Spirit would grow in that person and transform him, and health might even be thereby restored through the power of the Spirit. If full recovery is impossible, the patient can still receive the strength to bear the illness and suffering in the name of Jesus Christ.

This sacrament was formerly called extreme unction, and Catholic practice restricted its reception to those who were about to die. Thus the sacrament played an important part in our future, but it was not a frequent occurrence in parish life. The Second Vatican Council, in restoring the sacrament to its initial purpose and in changing its name, also changed the practice of its celebration.

No longer should a Catholic wait until he is on his deathbed before requesting this sacrament. We should celebrate the sacrament of anointing at the onset of any serious illness or before any major surgery. Also, the anointing may be celebrated more than once during a chronic illness, and old people are encouraged to receive the sacrament at various times—perhaps at Masses for the sick which are already being celebrated in many parishes.

Through the reforms of the Second Vatican Council, the sacrament of anointing is becoming a more frequent celebration in the Church. Our culture as a whole ignores sickness except when it can be cured, and we see no value whatsoever in suffering. Today the value of this sacrament lies not so much in its healing properties. This action calls us to regard sickness as a valid part of life with much to teach us concerning the meaning of life. Sickness can purify our priorities, crush our false idols, and direct us toward the ultimate concern of our existence: God.

Peter carries on Jesus' healing ministry in Acts 3:1-10.

James 5:12-20 indicates the presence of the ministries of reconciliation and healing in the apostolic Church.

 **The Church Praying**

Lord Jesus Christ,
you shared in our human nature
to heal the sick and save all mankind.
Mercifully listen to our prayers
for the physical and spiritual health of our sick
    brother
whom we have anointed in your name.
May your protection console him
and your strength make him well again.
Help him find hope in suffering,
for you have given him a share in your passion.
You are Lord forever and ever. Amen.

(Prayer from the Anointing of the Sick)

The Christian Prays

Tend your sick ones, Lord Christ;
rest your weary ones,
bless your dying ones,
soothe your suffering ones,
pity your afflicted ones,
shield your joyous ones,
and all for your love's sake.

(St. Augustine)

13

Sacraments of Christian Witness—
Marriage and Priesthood

Sacrament of love—Christian marriage

All human societies practice some form of marriage—a more or less permanent relationship between a man and a woman. The dominant symbol of
the relation is the act of sexual intercourse: the most
powerful expression of man's desire to unite with
another. Plato even suggested that originally men
and women were joined together as one creature
with four arms and legs. But they were separated
into two creatures and ever since they have been
striving to reunite with one another.

Sexual intercourse communicates human love. In
intercourse the man and woman give themselves to
one another. Such is not always the case, but we are
speaking now of the exemplar rather than the rule.
The total abandonment to the other person in the
bodily fulfillment of sex mirrors on the physical
plane the self-sacrifice to the beloved that true love
requires. Sexual intercourse serves as a symbol of
the couple's love at the same time that it strengthens,
deepens and promotes their love.

The prophets of Israel used the symbol of marriage to describe God. Yahweh was a bridegroom and Israel his bride. Seeing her in Egypt he had fallen in love. He chose her for his own, brought her out of Egypt, washed her clean in the Red Sea, and took her for his wife, to have and to hold forever.

But Israel had been unfaithful; she had played the whore. Chasing after other gods she forgot her marriage and what God had done for her. Again and again in the prophets God pleads with Israel to return, to honor her marriage. Hosea is commanded to illustrate Israel's situation painfully in his own life: he marries a prostitute who constantly deserts Hosea to run after other men. But again and again God asks Hosea to take her back and to forgive her adultery.

The tragic marriage of Yahweh and Israel should rightfully end in divorce. Israel frequently does not act the wife and bride. She deserts her bridegroom often, fickle to the core. But God on his part is faithful. He punishes Israel only to make her see her infidelity, only to coax her to return to her true home. Although he has more than enough cause, he will not give in to a divorce—Israel may abandon her home and lie with every idol she fancies. Yahweh still waits for her to return, ever ready to forgive her.

This symbol of marriage becomes one of the central metaphors of the Christian experience. Now however Christ is the bridegroom and the Church his bride. Jesus proves the extent to which God would go for his beloved—he gives up his life for her. Jesus cannot divorce his Church—he has given his promise and already made the ultimate sacrifice for her. Yahweh made marriage a relation of faith; Jesus adds the dimension of permanence to the marriage symbol. The human symbol of marriage is enriched and given fuller meaning through Yahweh and Jesus. God's love for man speaks of a union between two persons; it is a love faithful in spite of infidelity, a love willing to sacrifice, a love constant and permanent.

The Christian couple through their marriage are called upon to manifest in their love for one another the love of Jesus for this Church. Christian marriage becomes a school of love. True deep love is not easily come by. Most people enter marriage merely infatuated with each other or merely in love with love itself. But love is unreal until it is enfleshed. In marriage's school we learn slowly and often painfully how really to love one another. We are selfish and we are used to thinking of ourselves first. But when we marry we are no longer alone; there are now two of us wanting to be one. And this unity can only be learned in love. We must learn sacrifice. Only then can we truly know love. John says that the greatest love a man has is to give up his life for another—this of course is Jesus' love and he is the master in the Christian school.

Marriage is raised to a Christian sacrament because it is a unique opportunity to encounter Jesus Christ. The God who is love can be experienced in the human institution of marriage. As the man and woman grow in love for one another they experience Jesus in a very real way. Christian love is not some unearthly ideal, but the everyday love of one human being for another, and this love is focused in marriage.

The sacrament of marriage is not a once in a lifetime moment, present in the marriage ceremony. The marriage ceremony itself is merely a promise from the couple to enter into the sacramental relationship of marriage. The sacrament, the encounter with love, continues for the rest of our lives. In every expression of love Jesus is once again made flesh—given body. Christian marriage should extend Jesus' experience into every corner of human existence. Love radiates outward; it cannot be contained or bottled up: it demands to flow in giving. The love between husband and wife overflows in their love for their children, and if powerful enough it transforms their friends as well. The mission of Christian marriage does not speak of Christ's love: it *loves*. And love speaks louder than any words.

Inasmuch as Christian marriage is a growing in the love of Christ, an experience of the God who is love, it must also reflect the permanence of God's love. God did not forsake Israel and Christ will never divorce the Church. God's love is completely unconditional—he will not revoke it once it has been given. Jesus did not hesitate to live out to the end the consequences of his love—death on a cross.

Similarly a Christian marriage, if it is truly to participate in Christ's love, must involve total commitment, unconditioned by any reality other than death. Love can only exist and grow if there are no strings attached: I cannot really love you if I intend to quit loving should certain conditions not be fulfilled.

Today in our culture the institution of marriage has entered upon hard times. One out of three marriages ends in divorce. As Christians we share a ministry of healing and support to all those people who are ensnared in the tragedy of divorce. The divorced person is not a pariah and usually needs more than ever to feel through us the forgiveness, acceptance and love of God.

At the same time, however, we cannot, as Christians, ever compromise our ideals of marriage. Marriage is permanent, it is totally faithful, and it ordinarily gives birth and nurture to new life. Only if it fulfills these requirements does it reflect God's love for us. Nor can we afford to say that these are ideals that are impossible to fulfill in ordinary human life. We can never compromise these ideals, for only by following these conditions can the fidelity, the life and the love of God be experienced by the married couple, their children and their friends. It is through this sacrament of matrimony that the majority of people experience God, but the experience of God will be true and faithful only in a marriage entered into under these ideals.

We Catholics have a twofold mission with regard to marriage in our society. We must help those whose marriages fail and we must assure them that they are not cut off from either God or the Church. At the same time we must stress both for ourselves and our society the ideals of marriage, for only under these ideals can the true richness of the experience of marriage survive. Moreover, we must not only talk of these ideals and advocate them. We must also seek to provide support for those ideals in any way we can. There are many agencies today which enable couples to separate. How many agencies are there which try to help a couple live up to the ideals of marriage?

Love is not easily come by in our world—it is not similar to attraction or affection. It does not in the least depend upon some innate lovability in the person. No one is lovable until he is loved. A man and woman who marry do so committed to learn to love each other. Love cannot grow if they give up when the going becomes rough: only in the rough going can true love begin. Only in the rough going do we come to see our need for our beloved, our anguish in being alone: the truth that we were made for another and that we die unless united in love.

> Ezekiel uses the image of marriage to describe Israel in chapter 16. Hosea's story is in the first three chapters of his prophecy.
>
> Ephesians 5:21-33 compares the Church to the bride.

 **The Church Praying**

From the Marriage Ceremony

Father, all-powerful and ever-living God,
we do well always and everywhere to give you thanks.

You created man in love to share your divine life.
We see his high destiny in the love of husband and wife,
which bears the imprint of your own divine love.

Love is man's origin,
love is his constant calling,
love is his fulfillment in heaven.

The love of man and woman
is made holy in the sacrament of marriage,
and becomes the mirror of your everlasting love.

Lord, may all married couples praise you when they
    are happy
and turn to you in their sorrows.
May they be glad that you help them in their work
    and know that you are with them in their need.
May they pray to you in the community of the
    Church,
and be your witnesses in the world.
May they reach old age in the company of their
    friends,
and come at last to the kingdom of heaven.

Amen.

The Christian Prays

O blessed Lord,
you have commanded us to love one another;
grant us grace that,
having received your undeserved bounty,
we may love everyone in you and for you.
We seek your clemency for all,
but especially for the friends
your love has given us.
Love them, Wellspring of love,
and make them love you with all their heart,

that they may will and speak and do
those things only which are pleasing to you.

(Anselm of Canterbury)

Sacrament of service—Christian priesthood

Jesus preached the centrality of love, and his actions taught that love finds fulfillment in service. This experience was entrusted to a select group of men, his disciples. These men were responsible for bringing the good news to the world. They serve God for the sake of men and men for the sake of God.

Priesthood is a structure found in all man's religions. The priest acts as a bridge between his fellow men and God. He is a mediator. He offers sacrifice to God in the name of his fellows; he oversees and performs the sacred ritual by which the religious experience is conveyed; he preserves and protects the religion from deformation and corruption. He pleads on behalf of the people to God: he asks for rain so that the crops might grow, prays over the sick for their recovery, asks for victory in battle. Because of his sacred duties he is a special person—holy, dedicated to the things of God.

Israel began to distinguish between the various functions of the priest. In her early days she too had a priestly office. But the prophets saw Israel itself as a priestly people. Israel stood before God; Israel received God's Word for men. Israel herself was different from the other nations—holy and dedicated to God.

When Israel was freed from her bondage in Babylon and allowed to return to her land, her conception of her priesthood grows. The Isaiah of the exile sees Israel as a priestly people because she mediates God to men. And in the strange and beautiful "Songs of the Suffering Servant" Israel herself becomes a priestly sacrifice to God on behalf of the nations. God works through Israel for all men: Israel is the light of God meant to dispel every man's darkness.

But Israel never fully realized her priesthood for the nations. This strand in her self-concept never came into prominence. Not until Jesus does it burst into blossom. Very early Christians saw in Jesus the Suffering Servant, the one who takes upon himself all our burdens, divisions and sin. He offers himself to God on our behalf, and his life becomes a sacrifice through which man and God are brought together.

Jesus is the one true priest because he is the true mediator. Really man and really God, he forms the bridge between God and man: making the divine human and the human divine. He offered himself in sacrifice to God on the cross. Unlike Israel he was obedient to God even to his death. He fulfilled perfectly the old covenant with Israel. And because he completed it he himself became the new covenant. This new contract cannot be broken because it has already been perfectly fulfilled in Jesus. It does not depend upon our work but upon his work accomplished on the cross. We have but to incorporate ourselves into Jesus in order to enter into this new contract. We have but to believe in him to be saved.

Baptized into Christ's body we become part of that body. As he was the priest of the world, so every Christian shares in his priesthood: the world encounters Christ through the Christian. The covenant sealed on the cross contains good news for every man—it contains man's freedom from condemnation and death, it unfolds the essence of reality: God's love. The Christian's priesthood brings this covenant to all men. For all must hear the good news that is theirs: the freedom and love they need not earn or labor for because it is given to them freely as a gift.

Such is the Christian's priesthood—to bring God to the world and the world to God. Christian priesthood is bestowed in baptism; in confirmation Christians are seated by the Holy Spirit and commissioned. They are reconcilers between man and God because man and God are *already fully* reconciled in Jesus Christ and man needs only to be brought to awareness of it.

The Christian community also needs special men to devote full-time service to the faith. At first Christians appointed men to be the disciples' helpers. Then teachers were needed to pass on the experience and the dogmas. Preachers were needed to proclaim God's eternal Word to men immersed in changing time. And ministers were needed to administer and oversee the sacramental aspects of Christian life.

Out of this practical necessity grew the cultic priesthood in the Church. This forms a special priesthood. These men devote their lives to the Church and the Christian people. They mediate in a certain way between God and his people inasmuch as they teach the faith, preach the Word and administer the Church's rituals and sacraments. They exist to serve the Christian priesthood that belongs to every Christian, not to supplant it. They do not intervene between man and God but serve as instruments through which Christ's continuing work on earth is channeled.

The ministerial priesthood does not only serve a purely practical function, however. Like marriage it is a sacrament of Christian witness. The priesthood is a symbol through which a facet of Christ's vision becomes enfleshed in the world. Christian marriage is a focus for Christ's love: Christian priesthood becomes a focus for Christ's service.

Jesus taught his disciples that priesthood is an office of service rather than glory. The day before he died, John relates, he went around the dinner table and washed the feet of his disciples. In this action he caught the essence of Christian priesthood. Christ's ministers are not meant to be served but to minister to others. Christian priests do not live for their own sakes but for the sake of God's people. The minister gives up his own life to follow the example of the one true priest who gave up his life on a cross.

The sacrament of orders offers a man the challenge to encounter Jesus through a life of service and ministry. Just as Christian marriage enfleshes for the couple Jesus the lover, so Christian priesthood enfleshes for the minister Jesus the servant of all men. As Jesus existed for other men before himself so the priest puts on Jesus by dying to his selfishness and living for his people.

But priesthood is also a sacrament to all men. The priest accepts the duty and mission to show Christ the servant in his life. Assuming the office of priest he assumes the obligation to make his life transparent to Jesus. Men must be able to see Jesus the servant concretely present in the life of his priest. The priest strives to incarnate this aspect of Jesus into the world just as the Christian couple incarnates

Christ's love. Both sacraments carry this two-pronged significance: they allow the recipient to discover Christ in everyday life, and they also call the recipient to show forth Christ to the world in love or service.

Unfortunately Christians have often failed to realize these sacraments in their lives. Many Christian marriages do not proclaim love and are tortured with hate and selfishness. Similarly some Christian priests have sought power and glory for themselves rather than service to others. Christ's servant cannot wash his fellow man's feet in ermine robes.

But the failure of Christians and their distortion of the sacraments and of Christ's vision itself serves more to manifest the power of that vision than its weakness. How that vision could continue to illumine men in spite of the great distortions it has suffered through the centuries is a miracle. It is not so surprising that there have been Christian sinners but that in spite of their great abundance there have still been Christian saints. That Jesus' vision has not been lost or damaged through the sinfulness of his followers, that it has undergone resurrection after every crucifixion Christians have inflicted upon it, is surely a testimony of its truth and its power to prevail over our sinfulness and death. That an organization as corrupt as the Church can still produce holy men may be a sign of its divinity. God was perverse to choose to come among us as a mortal man. He has compounded the daring by remaining among us and working through sinful men and in a sinful institution.

Leviticus 8-10 gives the regulations for the priests in the tribe of Israel.

John 13:1-17 tells of Jesus and his demands upon those who would minister in his name.

The entire letter to the Hebrews develops the theology of Jesus' priesthood.

The Church Praying

Father,
you have taught the ministers of your Church
not to desire that they be served but to serve their
brothers and sisters.
May they be effective in their work
and persevering in their prayers,
performing their ministry with gentleness and concern for others.

(Opening Prayer for the Minister of the Church)

The Christian Prays

Lord Jesus,
help me to spread your fragrance everywhere.
Flood me with your spirit and life;
penetrate and possess my whole being so completely
that my life may only be a radiance of yours.
Shine through me,
and be so in me
that everyone
with whom I come into contact

may feel your presence
within me.
Let them look up
and no longer see me,
but only you, Jesus.

(John Henry Newman)

Part VI

The Social Institutions

of Christianity

Introduction:

Conversion from Barricades

to Freeways

The walls around the garden of Eden were strong, for they had to protect the garden from the outside world. The social institutions of the old Church were strong as well. They had been erected as a result of the Protestant Reformation when the Church had been forced to fight for her life. The Church of the last four hundred years has been in a state of seige, assailed first by the Protestants, then by the newly emerging nations of modern Europe, and finally by the explosion of modern thought and science.

However, the fathers of the Second Vatican Council decided that a different view of the Church's position in the world better coincided with the vision of Jesus. They saw the Church existing in order to be of help to the world, rather than to save a few people from the world. They saw Jesus as a man who lived for others, and they called the members of his body to also live their lives for their brothers and sisters. They blew the blazing trumpets of the gospel message and the walls around the garden of Eden came toppling down.

As a vision of life that is passed from person to person and from generation to generation, Christianity cannot exist without substantial social institutions, for these institutions ensure that our vision of life is kept alive and successfully passed on. However, the institutions also exist to enable us to fulfill our commission from Jesus to share the good news with all peoples.

Our social institutions (our parishes, our schools, our hospitals, our pope) can no longer exist to protect us from the cold, cruel world. They now exist to help us serve the world and bring there the spirit of God. They no longer act like the barricades around the garden of Eden. Now they are freeways that circle and flow out from the city of Jerusalem. Today in our cities the freeways help to define our boundaries, but they also primarily exist to enable the inhabitants of the city to enter and leave easily. The freeways of the city bring nourishment and raw materials from the surrounding area into the city and then manufacture goods which in turn are returned to the surrounding countryside. Likewise the social institutions of Christianity serve the function of preserving the city in existence and of mediating between the city and its neighbors.

14

A Vision of a
New Jerusalem

The politics of God

Whenever three or more people come together for any length of time a committee inevitably develops. We are social animals: we cannot live alone. To be human we need to live with others, and our humanity, that which sets us above the animals, our thought and our language, arises out of our interaction. But if we are to live together some sort of structure is necessary. We quickly learn we are better off if each one does not proceed on his own. We are more successful if we hunt the animals together, if we grow our crops together, one man growing wheat, another potatoes, another apples. Some men are stronger and better able to defend the community. Some are better at getting along with people and are gifted with the art of governing.

As men group themselves into societies the structure of living becomes more complex and greater benefits become available than are possible in solitary existence. The social structure frees a man to exercise his particular talent and the society as a whole benefits.

Israel's God was a God of the nation, the human society, not a God of separate individuals. Yahweh is my God and he is also your God, but more, he is our God. He brings diverse men together into a nation, a society. He then rules and guides through the political activities of kingship, prophecy and law. For Israel, unlike Egypt and Babylonia, a person is a unique individual who must not be crushed in the mob but who can only become fully human and transcend toward the righteousness and holiness of God as a member of a society.

Yahweh is a God of politics and history. He is present in the marketplaces and battlefields of the world. He is not the abstract, intellectual God of the Greek philosophers: too pure to be involved in the transitoriness of human affairs. Yahweh does not shrink from dirtying his hands. And he finally immerses himself completely in the finite history of man. He becomes a man of flesh and blood, laughter and tears, energy and weakness.

Jesus differs not from Israel's God. The God who freed a group of slaves from Egypt and made them a nation, the God who abandoned that nation to conquest by the Babylonians, the Greeks, then the Romans, could be expected eventually to become inextricably involved in history. And he could do so only by becoming man.

Nor does God's involvement in history end with Jesus. There is no reversal to this un-God-like behavior. Through the incarnation God is irrevocably tied to our history—our daily living—the confusing, finite and intricate matrix of human affairs. The God become man in Jesus becomes a human society in Christ's Church. The God who took upon himself a human heart, brain, arms and legs, emotions and thoughts, has now taken upon himself all the structures of a human society.

Incredible to believe such an obviously human institution as the Church contains God on earth! But it is no more incredible than believing that a man shrieking in pain and suffering on a cross is God. The scandal of the Church is only the scandal of Jesus and the scandal of Israel continued. But as God's presence within history intensifies, the incredibility and the scandal increases.

Since the essence of Christianity is the experience and vision of Jesus, we can more easily understand why it should flow through a Church. Experience is only alive in people; it cannot be preserved in some book. The book you are reading now at best can only describe; it cannot give the full experience of Christianity: God works through man, he revealed his essence to us in a man, and we come to know him today through other people living in his vision and sharing his experience.

The bride and body of Christ

Just what is the Church, though? How have Christians understood themselves as a Church, a community of Jesus? Israel had seen herself as a nation dedicated to God. She was God's people on a pilgrimage through history, slowly wending her way toward history's end and the encounter with the God of history. Christians saw themselves as a continuation of Israel. The Church is the new Israel, the new people of God, who, although they continue the pilgrimage, yet have in Jesus the end of the pilgrimage already with them.

St. Paul develops two images of the Church in his letters. First the Church is the bride of Christ. Through the prophets God had spoken of his love for Israel: he had seen her in Egypt, had taken her to his heart and married her. Paul saw Jesus in a parallel relation to his Church: she is the new Israel, the bride he has ransomed by his cross and married forever.

But there is an even closer identification of Jesus and his Church in another Pauline image. The Christian community is Jesus' own body on earth today. All are members of this body which is led and governed by Christ, its head. All have various functions to perform, various talents to donate toward his body. Paul does not merely speak figuratively. In the truest sense of the word Christ is made flesh in the world today in the Church which confesses and believes in his name.

Steadfast faithfulness

Christians have Jesus' assurance that he is irrevocably committed to his Church. During his earthly ministry he chose the men whose duty it would be to carry his vision across the earth. He chose twelve men in particular and Peter to be their leader. To Peter he promised that come what may he would remain faithful to his Church, never abandoning her or divorcing her or allowing her to stray from him.

Christians gradually came to a deeper appreciation of this truth. When Christians talk of the infallibility of the Church they indicate Jesus' promise to stand by this community; he will not allow his people to fall away from him. His vision and experience will not die out or be lost in his community: until the end of time men will be able to come into contact with Jesus' experience, his victory, his outlook, through the Church founded on him. Inasmuch as Peter's successor in the Church's leadership, the pope, is the visible symbol of the community's unity and its continuity and identity with the original fellowship, the promise of infallibility rests in a special way with him. The pope becomes the abiding sign that Jesus' fidelity and protection rests with his Church.

Medieval pyramids

The stratification of society in the Middle Ages produced yet another image of the Church, this one basically hierarchical. Christians simply saw the Church in terms of her structure: a pyramid. The pope is the leader on top at the peak of the pyramid, then under him are the cardinals, then the bishops, then the priests, and finally, at the very bottom, the most numerous class, the people. This is a valid description of the Church's governmental structure, but it really does not approach the true nature of the Church. Imagine if the early Christians had based their understanding of Jesus on his physical appearance: he had long brown hair, brown eyes, was five feet eight inches tall and spoke with a Galilean accent. This nice description tells nothing really important about Jesus. It does not say who he is or why we follow him or what he offered to man. In the same way the pyramid image of the Church is inadequate because it says nothing truly significant. And many people were misled by the image: they thought that the pope was the essence of the Church, or perhaps the pope and the bishops, whereas in truth the essence of the Church resides in all Christians together. Today happily this pyramidal understanding is falling into obsolescence as a way of seeing the Church.

1 Peter 2:40-10 speaks of Christians as God's priestly people.

Paul sees the Church as Christ's bride in Ephesians 5:21-33 and as Christ's body in 1 Corinthians 12:4-30.

The Petrine promise is found in Matthew 16:13-20 and also in John 21.

The Church Praying

Lord,
hear the prayers of your people
and bring the hearts of believers together in your
    praise
and in common sorrow for their sins.
Heal all divisions among Christians
that we may rejoice in the perfect unity of your
    Church
and move together as one
to eternal life in your kingdom.

(Opening Prayer in Mass for Unity of Christians)

The Christian Prays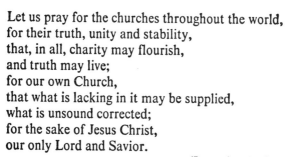

Let us pray for the churches throughout the world,
for their truth, unity and stability,
that, in all, charity may flourish,
and truth may live;
for our own Church,
that what is lacking in it may be supplied,
what is unsound corrected;
for the sake of Jesus Christ,
our only Lord and Savior.

(Lancelot Andrews)

The handmaid of the Lord

Recently Christians have begun to see in Mary, the Lord's mother, an image of the Church. Originally Mary's role helped come to an understanding of Jesus, but the recent shift in emphasis sheds much light on the Church. Pope Paul VI encouraged this development when at the end of the Second Vatican Council he proclaimed Mary the Mother of the Church.

During the first centuries Mary came to be recognized as the Mother of God. By this title the early Christians affirmed her motherhood of the whole Jesus, both his divinity and his humanity. Such a confession prevented a splitting of Jesus' personality —his divinity and humanity were indissolubly fused together. If Mary is the Mother of God because she brought the Savior into this world, then the Church can see herself as the Mother of God also, for Christ continues throughout the ages to enter the world through the Church. In her eucharist, her preaching, her mission and her witness the Church truly makes Jesus flesh in the world.

Mary was the culmination and flower of Israel, totally open and receptive toward God. Because of her role as Jesus' mother she was preserved by God free from sin throughout her life. When contemplating Mary's holiness and sinlessness the Church must see herself also as the handmaid of the Lord. For in spite of the sinful and disobedient members that make her up, she is the body and bride of Christ and she is holy and sinless because he is holy and sinless. Like Mary we as the Church are not made so because of ourselves but because we stand in Jesus who does make us so.

Finally a long Christian tradition says that Mary after her life on earth ended was taken immediately up into heaven. This tradition, just as the traditions of Israel and Jesus, is not a literal description of an event but rather a conveyer of truth concerning God, an experience of God. In the story of Mary's assumption i.e., her complete fulfillment in God, Christians see the conclusion of God's work in the world. At the end all creation will be drawn toward God and transformed in his light. In Mary's assumption the Church sees her own destiny and goal: she will not be abandoned but will be drawn up into union with God. The victory already won by Christ's cross will eventually penetrate and transform the entire universe.

Recently some Catholics have been disturbed over what they feel is a downgrading of Mary in Catholic life. Mary is still important, but in the future she will not play the role she assumed in popular piety in our recent past. In the old Catholicism Mary was a very popular figure because she embodied all that was loving, tender and humanly forgiving in our religion. Jesus, for most Catholics, had become so divine that he was almost unapproachable. In addition he was the judge before whom we would have to appear eventually, and, as God, he had to judge justly.

Our picture of Jesus has undergone considerable purification and renewal within the last decade or so. He now appears to us as much more human, and at least our children have no trouble finding him quite forgiving and merciful. We no longer feel a need to have Mary the mother protect us from the stern justice of her Son. We can now experience Jesus as a just man and judge, but also as a man motivated by love and mercy. Mary's symbolic role of the merciful one has once again shifted focus to Jesus. Thus Mary's prominence in our popular prayer life will decrease.

However, Mary is now taking on a new and different role. As the pre-eminent Christian, she is a sign for the Church. Her life and glorification can be read as a pre-figuring of the life and destiny of the Church.

As members of Christ's Church we are not what we once were. Once we were separated from our brothers and sisters in strife and division, sin and darkness. But now we are one because of Jesus. We still act sinfully though we have been freed from sin: we still die though death is dead. But as we, the people of God, march through history, we are called to make the vision penetrate more and more into our world. The seed of that vision takes root in our life and from us it is sown further afield until the whole creation has been transformed and becomes in act what it already is in deed in Jesus Christ.

Luke sees Mary as the epitome of Israel in Luke 1:26-38, 45-46. John sees her as the figure of the Church at the beginning of Jesus' ministry (John 2:1-12) and at the cross at the end of the ministry (John 19:25-27). The woman in Revelation 12:1-17 is also a figure of the Church and of Mary.

 **The Church Praying**

Father,
the image of the Virgin is found in the Church.
Mary had a faith that your Spirit prepared
and a love that never knew sin,
for you kept her sinless
from the first moment of her conception.
Trace in our actions the lines of her love,
in our hearts her readiness of faith.
Prepare once again a world for your Son
who lives and reigns with you and the Holy Spirit,
one God, for ever and ever.
(Opening Prayer for the Feast of the Immaculate
                                        Conception)

The Christian Prays

Lord, the whole assembly of the Church
sings out your greatness, our Redeemer,

The Christian Prays

Lord, the whole assembly of the Church
sings out your greatness, our Redeemer,
with the words of your Blessed Mother;
you looked with favor on your lowly handmaid,
both when the Virgin conceived you,
and when the Church acknowledged you by faith.

From Mary's womb
you came to redeem the Church;
therefore all ages call her "blessed,"
and in the Church all peoples find blessedness.

Lord, receive your people Israel;
remember your merciful promise made to our fathers,
and let that promise be fulfilled,
by the redemption of all the world.

Merciful God,
stand by your Church,
and continually purify your adopted children in her
bosom,
who, while enclosed in Mary's womb,
hallowed John in the womb of Elizabeth,
and who lives forever. Amen.

(Ancient Spanish Liturgy)

15

The Civics of

Incarnation

The flesh of permanence

Having seen how Christ works through his Church and how the Church sees herself, we now turn to the much more prosaic matter of Church organization. What is the machinery that keeps this institution running from day to day, from year to year? And first we must distinguish between the essential structures of the Church and the inessential, temporary and changeable elements. The former were given by Jesus himself in the early Church while the latter grew up as the result of some need during the course of the Church's life and could be replaced if they cease to serve a useful purpose.

Jesus' ministry was to the people of Israel, but a large proportion of his time was spent with a small group of men, twelve in all: his disciples. After his resurrection this group was sent to bring his vision to the rest of mankind. They were the authentic hand-picked transmitters of the Christian experience. From among the twelve Jesus chose Peter as leader: his office provided a center of unity for the disciples.

He was not appointed a dictator or a monarch or a king but a leader. His office was not of power but of service.

Catholics believe the office of the disciples passed on to their successors called bishops. These men are not equal to the apostles; still they are the leaders of the community which the disciples established. In Greek the word "episcopos" means overseer: the bishop is the leader and teacher of a certain community of Christians. In the bishop resides the fullness of the priesthood: he celebrates all the sacraments with his people.

The office of Peter as the head of the disciples also passed to a successor now called the pope. The pope is a symbol of Christian unity and continuity: he is a sign of the Church's oneness both in time and space. The bishops and the pope govern Christ's Church. They are not the head of the Church: that is Jesus himself. They are the caretakers of the Christian community upon earth. They are symbols of Jesus in the world: they must teach and live his vision of service to their fellow men.

The bishop is the leader of a diocese and he is the head of the Catholic communities in that area. To his people he is a symbol of Jesus. One of his signs of office is a shepherd's crook, for just as Jesus called himself the good shepherd sent to care for the sheep, so the bishop cares for the Christian people, Christ's flock, in the name of Jesus. He is the teacher of the Christian experience, he celebrates with his people the sacraments, and he governs the affairs and charities of his diocese.

Within the Roman Catholic branch of the Christian Church the requirement of celibacy has for a long time been associated with the priestly ministries of the Church. This requirement prevents ministers of the Church from entering into the sacrament of marriage. Today according to Latin Church law all bishops and priests are required to lead a life of celibacy.

As a result of the Second Vatican Council there are today two different kinds of deacons within the Roman Catholic Church. If a man undertakes the ministry of the diaconate with the intention of eventually serving as a priest, he is bound as a deacon to the law of celibacy. In the recent past this was the only type of deacon in the Western Church. However, the Second Vatican Council reinstituted the office of permanent deacon. The person undertaking this office may already be married before he is ordained to the diaconate. All of these laws of celibacy are purely Church laws, however, and it is possible they could be changed in the future should the Church so desire.

During the history of the Church at different times all of the bishops have come together in council to deliberate how the Church should respond to the pressing problems of the age. When they are in council together with the pope they form the highest legislative and teaching body of the Church.

Priests are helpers of the bishop and participate in his priesthood. (This is the reason the bishop ordains priests. Only the bishop holds the full powers of priesthood.) They work under him, helping to care for the needs of the Christian communities of his diocese. They preach the Word of God, teach the Christian experience, baptize, celebrate the eucharist, hear confessions, witness Christian marriages, anoint the sick and preside at Christian funerals. They see to the needs of individuals in their particular community called a parish. The parish priest is the Christian minister most individuals have contact with: he is their local leader and minister.

The third minister of the Church is the deacon. The deacon helps the priest by preaching the Word of God, baptizing, distributing communion, witnessing marriage and presiding at burials. This office fell into disuse during the past but today it is again revived because of the need for more ministers.

The changeable clothing of custom

The three offices of priesthood—bishop, priest, deacon—are the Christ-instituted ministries of service for the Christian community. But during the centuries other positions and organizations have grown within the Church to meet various needs. We can only mention a few in passing.

The pope has the privilege of appointing men to be cardinals. The office of cardinal is simply an honorary post within the Church. Any Christian may be honored by the office, although in fact cardinals today are taken from the body of bishops. Cardinals have only one official duty: they elect the pope.

Recently a number of eucharistic ministreis have again been brought into use within the Church. These ministries are undertaken not by the clergy but by lay men and women. These ministries all revolve around different roles assumed for the celebration of the eucharist and include readers, cantors, commentators and lay distributors of communion.

In the future, perhaps more areas of ministry will be
opened up to lay people. However, again it is important to stress that in essence every Christian is a
minister called to serve his fellows just as Jesus
served. The specialized ministries within the Church
are limited ministries of service to the Christian people and do not substitute for the larger ministry of
service to the world to which Jesus calls every one of
us.

There are groups of men and women in the
Church who are called religious. Gathered together
into different communities they exist either because
of a special work or mission or because of a special
way of life. For example the Paulists are American
priests working to mediate between American society and the Christian experience.

There are also communities of men known as
brothers and of women known as sisters or nuns.
These groups do special work such as teaching or
nursing, and the members live together a life of special Christian witness. They take three vows of chas-
tity, poverty and obedience as a special way of following Christ.

And the body—
poor, dumb brother ass

Most of us do not form one of these select and
specialized groups within the Christian community.
We are the body, not too distinguished—clumsy,
brother ass as St. Francis affectionately referred to
his carcass—but it is in *our* lives finally that the
vision of Jesus must take fire. All the administration

of the Church can really do is administer. They have never had any particular claim to holiness or sanctity. We the people are the body in which the vision of Jesus passes to the world.

And we the people live many different kinds of lives, all of which can be holy, all of which should find a home in the community called the Church. We are married, we are single. We are widowed, we are divorced. We are adolescents, we are the elderly. We are lame, we are dancers. We are black, we are white. We are homosexual, we are heterosexual. We are saints, we are sinners. None of us are worthy, yet all of us are loved.

The Church exists to embrace all varieties and cultures of men and women and there are an almost infinite variety of life styles open to the Christian. It is not that one is better than the other. Each Christian has a unique life, a unique story to tell: some may be called to serve the Church as bishop, others as a sister, others as a doctor or a housewife. The only important thing is that whatever the vocation, it is lived in the light of the Savior. Every Christian life is holy and sacred to the extent that Jesus can be seen in it.

The office of bishop is developed in 1 Timothy 3:1-7.

The deacon is mentioned in Acts 6:1-7 and 1 Timothy 3:8-13.

The priests of the community are referred to in 1 Timothy 5:17-25 and in Titus 1:5-9.

Paul speaks of the various gifts within

the Christian community in 1 Corinthians
12:1-31.

 **The Church Praying**

Father,
through his cross and resurrection
Jesus freed us from sin and death
and called us to the glory that has made us
a chosen race, a royal priesthood,
a holy nation, a people set apart.

Everywhere we proclaim your mighty works,
for you have called us out of darkness
into your own wonderful light.

(Preface for Sundays I)

The Christian Prays

Lord of the Church,
make us living communities
where your Spirit speaks and works.
And may I too be prepared
to give to the service of my community
the gift with which you endowed me.
Grant that I may serve the Church
not to win the esteem and approbation of men,
but out of truthfulness and love.

(Otto Reithmuller)

Part VII

The Experience of

Christianity

Introduction:

Conversion from Irrelevance

to Meaning

We are now approaching the heart of the new Jerusalem, the core that gives life to the city. What is it? It remains pretty much indescribable, and our experience of life as Christians still remains pretty much indescribable. Our vision resides in the words of our myths, the gestures of our worship, the conventions of our dogma, the actions of our ethics, and the structures of our institutions—and yet it lies beyond them as well. Perhaps we can only share this great joy we find in Jesus with other people by sharing our faith, our hope and our love.

Hopefully our journey has made us familiar with this strange, exciting city. We find here many similarities to the garden of Eden—we know the same God and worship through the same sacraments and believe through the same stories. But Jerusalem is a better place. It is more difficult to live here, but we feel closer to Jesus. We feel more a part of him and his vision. We will find here more meaning as we share in his mission.

Gardens are for children to play in. They are protected and isolated. As adults we move into the streets of the city where we engage one another in the adventure of the marketplace. Perhaps we felt our Catholicism was irrelevant because without knowing it we had outgrown the garden. As we take our place now among the concourse of humanity we shall find the words and visions of Jesus resonating deeper within our being and calling us to find him in the midst of humanity.

16

Christian Faith:

The Experience of Prayer

Paul once described Christian existence as a life of faith, hope and love. We can do no better than follow Paul as we discuss three central facets of Christian experience. We have already focused upon Christian experience throughout our investigation, for Christianity is an experience, and its stories, dogmas, rituals, ethics and social institutions are only the means by which we come into the presence of the experience and enter it. But faith, hope and love focus in a special way upon the experience of Christianity.

To walk in faith

As a man of faith the Christian believes in something: he holds something valuable and sacred. If need be he is willing to die for this faith, this belief. He is a committed man, with certain opinions and values. Meaning shapes his life. He does not drift; he has a goal and a purpose.

The Christian's faith is not in himself or another man or in nature or some impersonal force, but in a living and personal God. Only God gives meaning and purpose to life. Christians differ little from other men: they are not, as a lot, starry idealists or naive supernaturalists. For the most part they are a rather earthy lot. They live much as most people live, looking no further than necessary to find meaning. The clock stops ticking not because of God but because it needs to be wound. The sun rises not because God makes it come up but because the earth rotates. But behind the life of ordinary meaning there is a faith that we are not alone, that we are not in the unfeeling hands of an impersonal fate which cares not at all about us. Human and scientific meaning can be pushed only so far. Eventually we are confronted with an ultimate question. Is there any meaning outside of man and his fertile mind. Are we the only intelligence in the universe? Is love just a human consolation, a sentimental curse on a weak animal species? When a Christian pushes meaning to its outmost limit, he acknowledges in the end God.

No abstract God, the Christian God is concrete in the extreme. He is so individual he dared to take upon himself a human nature and to walk the earth at one point in time. No silent God, he speaks his Word into the universe and gives it meaning. He wishes to talk with man, to converse with him, enter into a personal relation with him. And Jesus' ministry taught us how to converse meaningfully with God, how to pray.

The man of faith is a man of prayer. He opens his inmost being to God, his most secret hopes, fears, desires and thoughts. A Christian cannot stand off, remaining on impersonal terms with God. He desires a union with God as close as that of a father and his son. He keeps nothing back; he gives himself freely in this dialogue, approaching his God with all his faults and his perfections, his weaknesses and his strengths.

Our Father in heaven

Christian prayer finds its perfection in the prayer Jesus gave his disciples, the Lord's prayer. This is the model for every Christian prayer to imitate. It begins with an address to God as our Father. God's fatherhood formed one of the central themes of Jesus' teaching. God is a Father to us and we should approach him accordingly. Naturally as a Father he is due our respect and reverence. But he is not forbidding or overly awesome either. Jesus elsewhere calls God "Abba" which means "Daddy": a term of endearment and intimacy. We need not be pretentious, we need not put on airs or a false formality. We need conceal no part of ourselves from him: we can be truly ourselves. God fully accepts us since he is Father.

Holy be your name

As our Father he is deserving of our praise and admiration, for he created all things. More powerful than anything we can imagine, he is beyond our every conception. He is mysterious and awesome as a father is to a small child. Because of the beauty of his creation, because of his love and care for us, we want to honor him, to praise him, to glorify him: holy be your name!

Your kingdom come

God promised to establish a kingdom, a nation of people joined together because of their union in God. Jesus came preaching the coming of God's kingdom. An ironic cut at the Christian religion is that Jesus came to bring a kingdom and the Church is what he got. The Church is not the kingdom, but the beginning of and the highway to the kingdom. We trust in the future kingdom of God because we have a foretaste in Christ's Church. The Christian believes in the kingdom and gives his life over to helping bring about the progressive realization of the kingdom on earth.

Christian faith looks toward the future. Great things have already happened in Christ, but now we must look forward to the fulfillment when the whole universe will be taken up into Jesus and presented to God as his kingdom. The kingdom is a vision and a goal, but through our efforts we can begin to build it not in daydreams but in human lives. Christian faith is optimistic: although alone man will fail and disappoint, still man in union with God can progress.

Your will be done, on earth as in heaven

In his will is our peace—not because God is anything like a tyrant or a dictator, but because his will accords with the nature of the universe. To follow his will means to be in harmony with man and creation. In his will lies the secret of our happiness.

The kingdom is realized through obedience to God's will. It is already here on earth in Jesus Christ through his total fidelity to God. In faithful obedience we do not lose our liberty and freedom. Rather only in the will of God can we achieve the freedom we were born for. We were born to love and be loved, to dwell in peace. And peace is ours only if men put off their selfishness and pride for the selflessness and humility seen in Jesus. We were born for beauty not ugliness, for harmony not discord. And to create harmony any composer will say that all the voices must follow a higher vision than their own individual melody. The individual strand of melody is not lost but blends into the greater beauty of the whole.

The kingdom implies a harmony among men, achieved only if all follow the will of a higher power. In his will is not only our harmony and our peace, but life itself. In the beginning, said the Israelites, God created the world out of chaos. Into confusion he brought order and harmony. John says the Light which is God entered the darkness and shone in the darkness. Creation is not over; God is still creating today. Into the chaos and confusion of human beings he brings order and harmony. Amid the destruction and wars of nations he is building a kingdom of peace. In our darkness a light has pierced whose name is Jesus. In the light may we do his will.

Give us today our daily bread

It is fine to honor God and to pray for such ideal and abstract realities as his kingdom, but many of us feel just a little too sophisticated to pray for our daily bread. We are twentieth-century men, far removed from the superstition that saw behind every happening the finger of God. God may have created the universe but he is not directly responsible for the thunderstorm which threatens me with its lightning. Why should I pray that he protect me?

Yet God did not shrink from being born a man; he has entered into the very real and particular world we inhabit. Our daily bread *is* his concern. Through such simple requests a Christian comes to know God and his will. We are like children who must grow up by continually asking questions: "Can I do this? May I have this apple?" If a child did not ask questions he could never grow into adulthood.

Our childish prayers to God are a school in Christian adulthood. They provide the opportunity to know God and ourselves as well by speaking to him of our deepest concerns. The way in which these prayers are answered shows us how God's will is taking shape in our lives. From infancy to adulthood, whether physically or spiritually, is a hard, long process.

God is no refuge when all else fails. We learn his will and his peace day by day. And we grow by the common bread he feeds us. But our daily bread is not only the mundane course of our lives: it is also the daily bread of the eucharist. For here our true daily bread is found: the bread which nourishes us and makes us grow in the knowledge and love of

God. In God's Word heard there and in the example of Jesus played out there daily we discern God's will in our life. This eucharistic prayer which is Jesus himself is the center of Christian faith.

Forgive us our sins as we forgive those who sin against us

The kingdom is built upon forgiveness. Forgiving sins was a prominent aspect of Jesus' ministry and it continues as a highly visible characteristic of his community. God's kingdom is not approached through revenge or retaliation but through forgiveness and reconciliation. Harmony in the Church is not won without dissonance: the kingdom is built not by saints alone but by sinners who may become saints, nor can it survive unless it is humbly forgiving.

Our model again is Jesus who said that if someone should slap you on the face the only response is to turn the other cheek. Christians believe this to be so even though they often fail to live up to it. Our faith is in a God great enough to forgive any wrong. If we would be like him we too must have faith in the power of good over evil, in the victory of charity over vengeance. Retaliation destroys itself. The only way out of the vicious circle of sin and wrong is complete forgiveness. In Jesus all of us have been forgiven by God; can we not now forgive one another?

**Do not bring us to the test
but deliver us from evil**

Our faith is not knowledge but trust and love. Its opposite is not unbelief but despair. Faith is not a philosophy; it is a way of living, an approach to reality. It is not something to be proved: it can only be seen and acknowledged. It cannot be stored up, but must be lived day by day. It has no magic charm to ward off evil. We are still human beings and fall to temptation, the temptation to be selfish, to hold grudges, to look out only for ourselves.

We can be certain of God's love and forgiveness but we can never be certain of ourselves. So we pray not to be put to the test. We have a great treasure in our keeping, and we must live in fear and trembling lest we dishonor it. Luther once cautioned: pray as if all depended on God and work as if all depends on yourself. Although the victory has been won, as long as we are on earth we live mostly on this side of the cross; Easter still lies on the other side.

> Luke and John are the masters of prayer. Significant passages in Luke are 1:67-69; 11:1-13; 22:39-46.
>
> The final discourse of Jesus and his prayer are found in John 14—17. This sums up John's whole theology.
>
> 1 Timothy 2:1-8 shows the importance of prayer in the early communities.

 **The Church Praying**

Important Christian Prayers

The Lord's Prayer

> Our Father,
> who art in heaven,
> hallowed be thy name.
> Thy kingdom come,
> thy will be done
> > on earth as it is in heaven.
> Give us this day our daily bread
> and forgive us our trespasses
> > as we forgive those who trespass against us.
> And lead us not into temptation,
> > but deliver us from evil.

> > > > > > > Amen.

The Angel's Salutation

> Hail Mary, full of grace,
> the Lord is with thee,
> Blessed art thou among women
> > and blessed is the fruit of thy womb, Jesus.
> Holy Mary, Mother of God,
> pray for us sinners now
> > and at the hour of our death.

> > > > > > > Amen.

The Doxology

> Glory be to the Father,
> > and to the Son,
> > and to the Holy Spirit.

As it was in the beginning,
   is now, and ever shall be:
   world without end.

                                          Amen.

The Christian Prays ▰▰▰▰▰▰▰

Lord, make me an instrument of your peace.
Where there is hatred, let me sow love;
where there is injury, pardon;
where there is doubt, faith;
where there is despair, hope;
where there is sadness, joy;
where there is darkness, light.

O Divine Master,
grant that I may not so much seek to be consoled as
   to console;
not so much to be understood as to understand;
not so much to be loved as to love.
For it is in giving that we receive;
it is in pardoning that we are pardoned;
it is in dying that we are born again to eternal life.

                              (St. Francis of Assisi)

17

Christian Hope:

The Experience of the Future

Repent and believe!

The Christian faces toward the future. Jesus' message was of a coming kingdom rather than something already present. The kingdom is here but it is also still yet to come. The earliest Christians believed that Jesus would soon return to inaugurate the kingdom, and they eagerly awaited this second coming; for their age was one of crisis and apocalyptic. The present life for most was one of hardship and suffering. They looked forward to the end of the present era and the dawn of a new age when God would put conditions right.

These Christians were a people of hope: for the return of Jesus and the transformation of the world. They hope for an end to their present suffering, for the speedy consummation and fulfillment of history. They envision Jesus coming on the clouds as a great judge. Men would be brought before him and would be judged as to whether they had walked in the light or the darkness.

But this hope was not fulfilled. Perhaps they had misunderstood Jesus. Perhaps the end is not so imminent, and they will die before it comes. Already in the New Testament Paul corrected some of his communities for placing undue emphasis upon the time of the end. Christians slowly began to realize that the interim period might be longer than a few lifetimes. If Christianity were to survive until this postponed end it would have to rethink its place in the world.

If Jesus will come to bring the world to its completion within a few years, such things as Church structure or a Christian's relations with the secular world are of little concern. But if this community may last for a considerable time, then one begins to think about organization and working out a *modus vivendi* with the world. Had Christianity not done this it would have died out; that it did reorganize and rethink its vision was a sign and proof of its great vitality and spirit. From a religion primarily concerned with making men ready for the judgment day, it became a religion concerned to spread to the ends of the earth Jesus' vision in terms of life in this world. Very early Christians stopped hoping and waiting for the end to come and turned themselves toward the task of making Jesus enfleshed in the world.

Maybe another day

The last day was postponed, made more distant and individual. Rather than an occurrence rushing upon them, Christians saw the last day as a far-off point in history or, better, as the moment of their own death. As they meditated upon the end an elaborate series of images and concepts grew up: images of a final day of judgment, of the tortures of hell, of golden streets and angels' wings in heaven, of a place of purification for those not sufficiently holy to enter heaven immediately. This whole imaginative structure grows throughout the Middle Ages until it flowers in *The Divine Comedy* of Dante and *Paradise Lost* of Milton.

Today most Christians find it difficult to believe in places such as heaven, hell and purgatory because of the very concrete images which originally grew up in order to make these realities more credible to earlier Christians. But just as the Christian hope did not die out in earliest Christianity but was transformed into the vivid medieval images, so today the Christian hope is not dying but is once more being transposed.

Christians believe and hope in eternal life. Death is not the end. We believe in a man who conquered death and gives us eternal life. Today however we are more sophisticated and the concrete images of the afterlife such as flames and harps do not help our hope. We have a hope in the eventual triumph of God through Jesus over sin and evil. We have a hope that creation will end in peace and union rather than chaos and destruction. We have the hope that at death we shall be fulfilled rather than annihilated. The feeble love we have managed to ignite in this life will burst into flame, and our flame will be joined with all other men in the one fire of Jesus Christ.

Fellow traveler on that final voyage

As the Christian approaches the hour of death a priest should be called in to administer the "rite of the sacraments for those near death." These ceremonies include three sacraments in addition to other prayers for the dying person. First, the Christian makes a last confession of his sins and receives absolution and reconciliation with God. Second, the person is anointed with the oil of the sick. This sacrament provides the consolation of the Holy Spirit during final hours of sickness and suffering. Finally, the dying Christian receives holy communion which is now referred to as "viaticum" (an old Latin word for "that which goes on a journey with a person"). At this point the Christian is on his way home, and through the nourishment of viaticum his journey is made in the strength and the companionship of the Holy Spirit.

When the last rites are concluded, someone should remain with the dying person in his last moments, for, as our Jewish brothers and sisters say, it is not good to let anyone die alone. These last rites should not carry any element of terror or fear for the Christian. They exist to provide consolation and they should bring peace to his spirit, for death is not the end. In the last rites we are preparing for a journey over the sea of death in a good bark called hope.

With the revision of the last rites following the Second Vatican Council certain practices have changed. First of all, to emphasize that the sacraments are for the living, the Council restricts their celebration to those Christians who are still living. No longer will dead Christians receive these sacra-

ments. At first this practice seems cold-hearted, but perhaps we are still working under the assumption that the sacraments admit us to the kingdom. We saw in our discussion of baptism that this is not so. Sacraments are only valid as acts of the Church community. God is not restricted to his sacraments. A Christian without benefit of these last rites may pass away without the comfort and meaning that they provide in his dying moments, but he is in no danger of being excluded from the kingdom of God simply because he has not participated in these sacraments.

When a priest arrives after the Christian has died, the Church now counsels that he help the family pray over the body of their friend and relative. It is we the living who need consolation and meaning in the moments after death. The dead Christian has passed beyond the veil and no longer needs our consolation or sacraments. He is in the presence of his loving Father.

════════ **The Church Praying**

Lord,
you are the source of eternal health
for those who believe in you.
May our brother (sister)
who has been refreshed with food and drink from heaven
safely reach your kingdom of light and life.

(Prayer from Viaticum)

Death, where is thy sting?

To understand Christian hope we must examine
the many Christian symbols which have grown up
around it. Christians do not take these signs literally.
If one went up in a rocket ship one would not arrive
at heaven's gate. Rather the Christian symbolic language of hope is a way of speaking, feeble though it
is, about things beyond our imagination and ability
to comprehend. Images and concepts of heaven, hell
and judgment are vivid ways of pointing toward a
truth and a hope: they are not maps of any territory.

There is one earthly end for us all: death. There is
no way of avoiding it: it is the lot man was born to.
Each society comes to a certain understanding of
death, and it learns to cope with death in certain
ways. It seems as though contemporary American
society denies the reality of death. Think how often
we use euphemisms to avoid confronting death head
on: "he passed away" rather than "he died" is only
the most obvious example. How the very word
"cancer" sends a shudder through our society! For
cancer inevitably means death. Instead of "corpse"
or "body" we refer to the "loved one" and the room
where the body is displayed is the "slumber room"
as though it were not dead at all. Men only joke
about those matters they take most seriously; today
we have an abundance of sexual or religious jokes
but how many stories of death are there? America is
afraid to confront this very present reality. We are
unwilling to "bury" our dead; instead we provide
them with "perpetual care."

Nothing could be farther from an authentic Christian attitude toward death. For the early Christians

death was a fact to be faced, but it held little true terror. For these men had already died in baptism and had risen to eternal life. Physical death was merely the final stripping away of what was earthly, the final bursting forth into the light.

Before the judgment seat

As the expectation of the world's end receded farther into the distance Christians began to think of their own individual death in terms of this last day. In my own death I pass over into eternity and encounter my Lord. The judgment of men is moved from the end of time to the end of each man's time.

But why should there be any idea of judgment? Is not the Christian experience that men are already justified? While this is perfectly true there is still the importance of history and the problem of human freedom to be accounted for.

Both Israel and Christianity experience God becoming most real to men in their history. Christianity cannot deny or denigrate history, for there salvation is worked out. Because man's deliverance from sin and death was accomplished upon the cross does not mean that it is unimportant what happens now. The victory won on the cross must penetrate into the entire fabric of history so that all of creation may be transformed and saved.

The Christian is not absolved from the task of history. He must appropriate the reality of his deliverance into his own life. To a Hebrew to know the truth was equivalent to doing the truth. A Jew knew God not if he intellectually acknowledged God's existence. Rather he knew God only if he was obedient to God in his life. Similarly, although we are rescued totally by Christ, still it is our mission to let Christ leaven our life. To be saved is not just a fact, it is a truth to be lived.

Christians take life seriously because in human lives and history God works. Our life shows the measure of our assimilation to Jesus' vision. As a man acts, so does he truly believe; if we believe the world is built on a loving God so we must act.

Although we are saved we live our lives in fear and trembling because of our great commission. And our death is the climax of our life: what we are then sums up our entire existence. From death we pass into the light of God. In his light our faults and failures will be shown up. We will show our belief by the story we have told. "Have you done the truth?" Such is the question awaiting every man.

Obviously most of us are guilty. We are lukewarm rather than on fire with the vision. Our lives have not been transparent to Jesus; at best we have been like smoked glass. Are we to be lost? Should we live in Christian fear rather than Christian hope?

The geography of eternity

In the days of persecution it was fairly easy either to be a Christian or to fall away. And the communities had to decide how to deal with those who denied the faith under pressure. Should the Church be just or should she be merciful? It was a momentous and extremely important decision. For it would determine whether Jesus' vision was for all men or for the few strong enough to incarnate it into their lives.

The decision fell in favor of mercy. Men who had failed were to be forgiven and received back into fellowship. But as the Church grew into a community containing many who were only nominal Christians, again the problem arose. But this time it arose concerning the final judgment. Would only the saints be united with God?

The earliest concepts of the next world pictured Jesus as judge, welcoming the good into heaven and condemning the evil to hell. But what of those men who were not great lights of virtue but not out and out villains either? Slowly the idea of a middle state arose. Those not yet ready to enter heaven went to a place of purgation where they were purified of the sluggishness toward God manifested on earth.

This doctrine of purgatory shows the concern of the Church to preserve the original Christian vision of God's mercy and forgiveness. If we are not good enough for heaven we need not be condemned to hell. Nor need we debase heaven's perfection and holiness by allowing sinful men a place there.

The experience of God's mercy is so overwhelming in Christianity that when during the Middle Ages Christ took on the primary characteristic of the judge on the Last Day, the Christian people through the figure of Mary preserved the experience of God's superabundant mercy. They felt that although Christ might condemn, yet Mary need never condemn and could plead with her son for the sinner.

Today the medieval over-emphasis upon Christ's judgment has been tempered by his mercy and the figure of Mary as the never-condemning pleader on our behalf can recede into the background. But that the Church should at one time have developed such a prominent role for Mary demonstrates the indomitable prominence of mercy and forgiveness within the Christian experience. Ours is to hope rather than to fear.

Unfortunately purgatory soon came to be understood quite literally. Originally none of the concepts of heaven, hell or purgatory were meant to be understood literally. They were not actual places; they merely represented relations to God.

Hell was the state that guaranteed man's freedom. For if every man were saved in spite of himself would he be free? Although God wishes to save everyone and draw him to himself, yet he will not violate man's freedom. Love may not be coercive. Man must be left the option to reject God. That state of closedness toward God is hell, and it is a Christian value judgment to call such a state hell. Christians say that the entirely self-sufficient man, the man who wills to live without love, is living in a state of hell. Fire and torture are merely images and are pale compared to the true pain a man inflicts upon himself through his selfishness.

Most men realize the value and need of love. Unfortunately in many ways they fail to live up to its demands in this life. They still have large areas of selfishness within them. They still grasp rather than give, whereas love is not love until it is given away. As these men grow in love they come closer to God. And their growth does not stop with death. For at death they will see God and the sight of God's love will burn away all of the selfishness and egotism remaining in us. The blinding and piercing sight of Love itself will wrench us away from our self-centeredness. We will be drawn unswervingly into the love which is life. Purgatory is no prison where most of us spend a sentenced amount of time. Purgatory is an image, like hell, to describe a way of life not only after death but this very minute. It should be the image of our life right now.

There are some men and women who have made their lives open to God; these are the saints, and at their death they join in full union with the object of their love. The state of this love is heaven. For most of us heaven is only a vision, a distant goal. Our life is a purgatory, not a heaven. But the idea of heaven shows us and keeps before us the hope that purgatory is only temporary. Heaven is everyone's final goal.

Heaven, hell and purgatory are three ways of living right now; they are three possibilities of human existence. Thus they are more than curious speculations concerning something we can never know this side of death. Our Christian life is lived in hope—a hope of heaven and a hope of God's infinite mercy. For his Church that would not expel sinners nor condemn men to hell hopes and lives in the faith that a God who loved man so much as to become a man in order to reach man will in the end again let his mercy triumph.

In the eucharist, the center of our Christian life, there is a real initiation of the Christian hope. In this sacrament God himself is offered to us in order to bring us into union. And he offers himself only on condition that we acknowledge our sinfulness and unworthiness. Before receiving the host we say, "Lord, I am not worthy to receive you, but only say the word and I shall be healed." We do not need to be perfect; we can acknowledge our faults. And our confession is met not by a refusal but by the giving of God into communion with us. Here is a foretaste of our hope of fulfillment: here is the true image of our God.

> Matthew 24 and 25 gives Jesus' discourse concerning the second coming and the Christian's attitude toward it.
>
> Paul talks to his community at Thessalonica about the return of Jesus in 1 Thessalonians 4:1—5:11 and in 2 Thessalonians 1:1—3:5.
>
> The final consolation of the Church is seen in the beautiful description of the heavenly Jerusalem in Revelation 21.

 **The Church Praying**

From the Service of Christian Burial

Father, all-powerful and ever living God,
we do well always and everywhere to give you thanks
through Jesus Christ our Lord.

In him, who rose from the dead,
our hope of resurrection dawned.
The sadness of death gives way
to the bright promise of immortality.
Lord, for your faithful people life is changed, not
    ended.
When the body of our earthly dwelling lies in death
we gain an everlasting dwelling place in heaven.

May we then go forward eagerly to meet the Lord,
and after our life on earth
be united with our brothers and sisters
where every tear will be wiped away.

Amen.

The Christian Prays

O Lord,
support us all the day long of this life,
until the shadows lengthen,
and the evening comes,
and the busy world is hushed,
and the fever of life is over,
and our work is done.
Then, in your mercy,
grant us a safe lodging and a holy rest,
and peace at the last.

(John Henry Newman)

18

Christian Love:

The Experience of God

God is love

Time and again we have found that Christian experience is an experience of God as love. But what is love? Love unfortunately has become sentimental and trite; it has been downgraded to mean no more than affection. Love is the substance of Hollywood films; it is not substantial enough to build a way of life upon. Christianity however says God is love; it does not say love is God. The Christian experience of God teaches us what love truly is; sentimental love does not teach about God.

Paul describes love in his first letter to the Corinthians. From him we can resurrect love from sentimentality. What is love? Love makes life possible. For without love I do not exist: I am empty, a shell with no substance. Any action I perform has meaning only in proportion to the love contained in it.

Love is the base and foundation of the human universe, the motivating principle, the ground of all reality. Man is only really man if he lives grounded in love. Everything else is secondary: faith, hope, good works, great accomplishments.

What is love? It is patient, kind, it does not envy. Love makes a man concerned for other men rather than himself. It decreases our egotism and our pride. Without love we will exalt ourselves; we will come to an overly high estimate of our importance. We think all is well if only we are well.

Love means a dying to selfishness. We are not righteous and good because of ourselves. If we can bear to look at ourselves objectively, we are full of faults. We should not be "quick to take offense" when rebuked because, being human, we probably deserve to be rebuked. We are righteous and good because of God's love for us which makes us so.

"Love keeps no score of wrongs." Love is forgiving rather than revengeful. It realizes and accepts our human frail condition. If things go wrong, if a friend slights me, if my wife fails to meet me downtown on time, naturally I grow angry because I have been treated ill, and naturally I know that I deserve better treatment. It is not just, and I shall take steps to correct this injustice against me.

But "let him without sin cast the first stone." Can I, an unjust man, in good conscience condemn injustice when my own injustice has been forgiven, totally and unconditionally, in Jesus Christ? What now can I do against the injustice committed toward me? Retaliate? Seek revenge? The justice and righteousness of Jesus retaliated against Peter's denial on Holy Thursday by seeking Peter out to forgive him and commission him to head the new community on Easter Sunday. Can we who stand in Christ do less? Love "does not gloat over other men's sins, but delights in the truth."

To be selfless, humble and forgiving is difficult—even impossible, it seems. It is easier to hold a grudge, or even to be sentimentally forgiving, than it is to love responsibly. We can not toss off forgiveness with a quick, "Oh, it was nothing." Love is responsible; it must be serious. If our brother has wronged and hurt us, we can not play the stoic and pretend that he has not touched us. Love calls us to respond to the hurt by opening ourselves even more to him. To love someone we must give ourselves over to him, and it is very difficult to make oneself vulnerable a second time. But how else can we understand the counsel to turn the other cheek?

We have only Paul's assurance that "there is nothing love cannot face." Somehow in Christ we can find the strength to respond to hatred with love. Although love seems so fragile, so wispy, so delicate, yet in Jesus' commitment in love even to the acceptance of the cross we see that "there is no limit to its faith, its hope, its endurance."

Love revealed

Christian love is based upon the most concrete exemplar possible. God shows us what love is: he loved the world so much that he gave his only Son so that the world might be brought into union with God. And the Son's example of love was to the extent of laying down his life so that we might be able to have life.

The perfect model of love is the Godhead itself. Jesus taught that God is our Father and is best spoken of as Love. The proper response to the Father's

love is to do the Father's will. We can see this in ordinary life: to show his wife how much he loves her,
the husband may take her on the vacation she has
always wanted to go on. He says, "I love you enough
to do gladly what you wish rather than what I might
want." True love willingly sacrifices itself. Jesus'
love for the Father involved such total obedience
that he did not shy away from the torturous death of
crucifixion.

In Jesus' resurrection the disciples came to experience Jesus himself as God. They saw him as the
bridge between God and man. Jesus is the true approach to the Father, and Christian prayer has
always been spoken to the Father through Christ our
Lord.

But the love between the Son and the Father is so
concrete, so real, so life-giving that it too can be understood only as a person. This love is so powerful
that it too has a separate existence. It is the third
person of God which Christians call the Holy Spirit.
The Holy Spirit within us draws us into the very
Godhead itself.

Love compels the lover to be open to others. True
love never shuts out anyone or anything. Marital
love grows through the addition of a child to the
family. If real love exists between the parents, there
can be no jealousy over the child. The love between
the two naturally radiates outward to include others
within the orbit of that love. The two lovers who
exist only for each other and who cannot stand the
intrusion of the world into their "love" are at best
infatuated with one another, not in love.

The love between the Father and the Son which
takes personal form in the Holy Spirit is sent forth

to bring the entire creation within the orbit of that Love. When we realize that the Holy Spirit is the core of the Godhead, we see the great dynamism of God. His very essence is to go continually out of himself, to create and bring the creation back into himself.

In baptism and confirmation Christians receive within themselves the very Holy Spirit of God. And the early Greek Fathers of the Church described the Christian's life as a divinization of man. As the Spirit comes to control and to permeate our life, we become more and more Godlike ourselves.

Oh happy fault!

The ancient Hebrews told a story of the first man and woman, Adam and Eve. God placed them within a garden of Eden where grew everything needed for their life and well-being. But God forbade them to eat the fruit of one tree in the garden—the tree of the knowledge of good and evil. One day a serpent approached the woman Eve and tempted her to eat the forbidden fruit. "God would not want you to eat that fruit because then you too would be a god," whispers the serpent into Eve's ear.

And Eve, tempted to become like God, did eat the fruit and persuaded her husband Adam to eat the fruit as well. Unfortunately they did not become like gods; they became like the men we know, men who do not live in any paradisical garden but rather amid the thorns and pain of human existence.

Originally God meant man to be fulfilled and to be happy as a creature of God in union with him.

But man was free and he chose to try to be like God by being equal to and independent of God. This first pride became rooted in the very nature of man, so that as man he is compelled to exalt himself as a god. But because he is a man he ultimately fails miserably.

God could have abandoned man to his fate and his misery of unfulfilled pride, but he did not. Man in the beginning went against the creator's plan for creation; he disobeyed and brought failure upon himself. The new initiative must lie with God.

Of course God might have shown man the way back to the proper position of humanity, and we could say he did this through Israel's law. But if he were to rescue man truly, somehow God must surpass even himself. What if he should fulfill man's original sinful desire to be like the gods? What if in order to make man like God, God should dare to become man?

God's reply to man's free act of disobedience in Adam is seen in Jesus Christ. Jesus is the second Adam who does obey God. But he is more. In him we actually are drawn into God as equals. God became man so that man could become God. Had man not sinned he would have lived as God's favorite creature, and he would have lived happily under God. But man's sin has shown clearly the extent of God's love. In Jesus we have more than we had in Adam, for in Jesus we have given to us the Holy Spirit who truly makes us like God. In the light of Jesus we can truly consider the fall of Adam happy because it has let shine upon us the brightness of God's love. Our disobedience is responded to out of all measure by the gift of God in Jesus.

The Trinity

The Trinity is the essence of Christianity because in the Trinity we find love's true nature, for God, although he is one, is yet three persons. The Father, the Son and the Spirit are all one in that they are God, but they form a dynamic rather than a static unity. The essence of God and therefore the essence of Love is sharing in union. The Trinity will always remain a mystery for us. We humbly acknowledge three persons in the one God. We confess that God is Father, Son and Holy Spirit while at the same time we confess that there are not three Gods, only one.

The doctrine of the Trinity is no idle speculation. It has an intimate relation to the Christian life. For the Christian through Christ and in the Holy Spirit is drawn into the very center of God into union with the Father. If the Christian comes to experience the three-in-oneness of God, he also comes to see the tri-une-ness of love. Love unites into one what was before separate. In the love of Jesus men come to understand that they cannot live alone. They are called to join with one another in love which is the creative and life-giving Spirit of God ever going out to embrace all creation and returning into the union of the Father.

In Jesus Christ lies our true destiny. We began with a question of meaning and of purpose, and we have found that question satisfied. Our heart has searched and questioned and been restless until it found that for which it was made. Our search ends only when we come to the home we are seeking and embrace the Father who, while we have been seeking Him, has been ceaselessly searching for us.

God's love for us is seen in Luke's parables of the prodigal son (Luke 15:11-32) and the good samaritan who is a figure of Christ (Luke 10:29-37).

Paul's hymn to love is in 1 Corinthians 13.

But the master of God's love in the New Testament is St. John whose first letter should be read in its entirety.

 **The Church Praying**

The Easter Hymn

Rejoice now, all you heavenly choirs of angels.
Rejoice, all creation around his throne
   for this mighty King is victorious.
Sound, O trumpet, tell of our salvation.
Rejoice too, O earth: you are made brilliant by such splendor.
   Rejoice, for you have been illumined.
   Darkness everywhere has been overcome by the brightness of this everlasting King.
It is truly right and just that with all the ardor of our hearts and minds we should proclaim with our voices the invisible Almighty Father and his only begotten Son, our Lord Jesus Christ, who paid the debt of Adam for us to his eternal Father, and with his precious blood washed away the penalty of original sin.
This is the night which restores to grace and unites in holiness those who believe in Christ, separating them from worldly vice and the darkness of sin.

This is the night on which Christ burst the bonds of
death and victoriously arose from the grave. For
life itself, without redemption, would be of no
avail to us.

O wondrous condescension of your mercy towards
us!

How far beyond our understanding is your loving affection, that you would ransom a slave at the price
of your Son.

O necessary sin of Adam, which was blotted out by
the death of Christ

O happy fault, that merited such a redeemer.

O truly blessed night which alone deserved to know
the time and the hour when Christ arose from the
grave.

The holiness of this night banishes wickedness and
washes away sin and restores innocence to those
who have fallen.

It puts hatred to flight, brings peace and humbles
pride.

It is of this night that Scripture says:
"And the night shall be as bright as day.
And the night shall light up my joy."

The Christian Prays

Bless all who worship thee,
from the rising of the sun unto the going down of the
same.
Of thy goodness, give us;
with thy love, inspire us;
with thy spirit, guide us;
by thy power, protect us;
in thy mercy, receive us now and always.

(Ancient Collect)

Epilogue:

Other Cities, Similar Journeys

We have now completed our exploration of the vision of Jesus as experienced and lived by the Catholic community of Christians. However, the Catholic vision of life is only one of many different visions. There are theoretically as many different experiences of life's meaning as there have been people on the face of this old earth. Such is potentially the case; actually, however, the number of all-encompassing visions is not so large.

How does the vision of Jesus relate to other conceptions of human existence? How does Christianity regard, say, the vision of the Buddha? How is the Christian different from the modern person who professes no organized religion and who claims to be an atheist? And within Christianity itself, how does the Catholic vision of Jesus differ from that of the other Christian communities?

These are important questions entailing huge consequences. For historically, and still today, many Christians regard all non-Christians as lost. Such an attitude has led in the past to bloodshed and still errects barriers to communication and understanding in our world today.

In this epilogue, therefore, let us explore the way in which the Roman Catholic Church views and relates to other religions, and let us also examine how she sees other Christian communities. The attitudes described here are only those of the Roman Catholic Church, and they do not necessarily coincide with the views of other Christian churches who may possess quite different outlooks on these questions.

Let us go up to the house of the Lord!

Throughout this book we have looked at man's religious nature in terms of a search after meaning. Whenever a human being seeks after meaning he is acting religiously. The religious questions initiate a journey. There are a multitude of pilgrims, but we are all on similar pilgrimages. Our quest is the same —a meaning to human existence. In this very basic sense Christians are no different from Jews, Buddhists, Muslims, atheists, philosophers or humanists; we are all pilgrims toward the city of meaning. The religious man differs from the non-religious man (if indeed there is such an animal) in that the non-religious man does not seek any meaning to his life; for him life is irrational, incomprehensible, without reason or truth.

Christianity as a religion is a response to our question of meaning. Jesus' life and teachings, death and resurrection respond to the deepest questions about meaning that spring from our spirit. But Christianity is only one possible response. There are an infinitude of others.

Unfortunately, Christianity as well as her mother religion, Judaism, and her sister religion, Islam, has a past history of intolerance for other religions. If one religion is true, the easy conclusion is that all others must be wrong. Thus soon after the Christian Church was born she turned on the Judaism that gave her birth and began the Christian persecution of Jews that ended only after the horror of Nazi Germany.

Only recently has the Roman Catholic Church come to a new, official understanding of the other faiths of mankind. Other religions are like our own, journeys toward meaning and God. And although the other pilgrims travel toward different cities with exotic names such as Mecca or Delhi, and although the geography and customs of these other cities may seem foreign and strange, nevertheless it does not necessarily follow that all these people are not our brothers and sisters. At this time, on this earth, it is the pilgrimage rather than the shrine that is important. Perhaps when we reach our destination (beyond the veil of this life) we shall find that our goals were in truth the same and that they only seemed different due to our human limitations.

We have emphasized again and again that the heart of any religion is not its stories, dogmas, rituals, ethics, or social institutions, but its experience. Experience is notoriously intangible and always just a little beyond the grasp of our words, thoughts and gestures. People of different faiths find great variations and even contradictions when they compare their stories, rituals, and the other components of their religions, but if they manage to move beyond to the experience, they often find that their different visions appear quite harmonious with one another.

Buddhism, for example, seems on the surface to be a very pessimistic religion. It preaches that exist-

ence is suffering, and it says that the only way out of
suffering is to destroy the self so that one ceases to
exist. To a Christian such a teaching goes contrary
to our vision of the kingdom of God which we believe will include the gift of fullness of life.

However, when Christians and Buddhists move
beyond their conflicting doctrines, the experiences of
people in both religions do not seem antagonistic or
discordant. Thus indeed it could conceivably happen
that we shall discover that Nirvana and the kingdom
are but different names for the same experience. But
such knowledge will only come with full enlightenment. When the kingdom of God comes with power,
and when the last blade of grass achieves Nirvana,
then we shall know in truth. To say anything now is
mere foolishness, and unfortunately Christianity has
in its history been given to much foolish chatter.

The universality of the kingdom

But does Jesus make any difference? From a
Christian viewpoint is it just as good to be a Budd-
hist as a Christian? Certainly the tradition of Christianity has not held that religion is indifferent. Christianity has had a great deal of bloodshed in its
history for the simple reason that it regards itself as
the true religion, and so from a Christian viewpoint
Jesus obviously does make a difference. As modern
Christians we must ask ourselves exactly what kind
of difference Jesus does make.

Jesus focused his teaching around the kingdom of
God. His requirement for entrance into the kingdom
was not so much belief in him as caring for our

brothers and sisters. Thus he made love for others the primary prerequisite for the kingdom. Christians should therefore have no trouble admitting all kinds of people into the kingdom, including Jews, Buddhists, atheists and agnostics, so long as these people have tried to love others.

Christians know about the kingdom of God, and this knowledge differentiates them from other people. Christians know the requirements for membership in the kingdom, and they continue Jesus' ministry by living their lives as signs that the kingdom of God is truly among us. Christians are called by Jesus to spread the good news, but this mission does not mean converting the world to Christianity. It involves helping all peoples to bring about the kingdom of God. The Christian encourages and inspires others concerning the kingdom through life and example rather than by preaching and argument. Thus the Second Vatican Council encourages Christians to help all peoples appreciate and live up to whatever is good in their own faiths rather than try to convert them to Christianity.

The Word among the words

The uniqueness of Jesus lies not so much in the fact that only in this man can be found the path to salvation, but in the truth that in this man is the path to salvation expressed most perfectly. We have seen how hard it is to capture experience in words, and religion attempts to respond to the deepest question we can ask: What is the meaning of it all? If it is difficult to convey adequately such very human experi-

ences as joy or sadness, is it any wonder that the
task of describing the power which guides the stars
lies so far beyond our stuttering speech?

The different faiths of mankind are attempts to
articulate this experience of meaning. This is a gar-
gantuan task, and all religions must be admired for
their accomplishment as well as their audacity. That
they have succeeded to some degree in awakening
this experience despite their frail words, faulty
dogmas, clumsy rituals and fallible institutions is at-
tested by their vitality today.

Among the various religions is there one that does
succeed in perfectly capturing the heart of the universe in human language? We Christians feel that in
Jesus this task is uniquely and perfectly accomplished. One of the favorite terms used by Christians to describe Jesus is the "Word." In Jesus the
experience at the heart of the universe took on a totally human form and spoke a human tongue, so
that if we wish to comprehend that experience in the
most perfect human words, concepts, and behavior,
we can do so in this man Jesus.

Thus from the Christian viewpoint Jesus and his
followers have no exclusive ownership of the experience of meaning, but Jesus does articulate the meaning of human existence better than any other human
being. For example, most faiths have some concept
of an afterlife. Now an afterlife, presuming there is
one, is certainly beyond the comprehension of all
human beings. No one has experienced it and lived
to tell the tale. Thus there are a number of concepts
used by the various religions to describe the afterlife.
The Indian religions rely on the idea of reincarna-
tion, while the Greeks often thought in terms of the

immortality of the soul. Christianity prefers the metaphor of the resurrection of the body. Now there is no denying that resurrection is still only a metaphor: it is a human concept used to describe an experience we as yet have no knowledge of. Naturally it can only point and hint concerning the afterlife; it cannot articulate that experience fully. However, as Christians we also believe that of all the different symbols and images used to describe the afterlife, this image of resurrection is the most adequate. There is no better, and the other images in some sense or other are ultimately misleading. Resurrection is therefore the most adequate image, and although it is not invented by Jesus, it is used by Christians and related to Jesus through his own victory over death.

The experience of God is common to many people, and yet it is beyond our capacity to grasp and comprehend. Jesus is the bridge between that experience and our intellect which shapes our vision of the world, the way we relate to each other, and our behavior in general. He is the Word of God made flesh so that we may behold the glory of God in our midst. Christians are by no means the only people on the great pilgrimage toward enlightenment and meaning, but we are the people who know adequately through Jesus how to express that ineffable experience using merely human language. This is the uniqueness of Jesus. Out of our confused babbling he shows us how to sing a song of truth and beauty. He delivers us from the darkness of limited human understanding and leads us to the light of God's radiance.

Discord among brothers

Once we Christians have understood ourselves in terms of the faiths of other people, we have only completed half the task, for the scandal and sin of the Christian community is that it is gravely divided against itself. Much of the faith of Catholics is the same as the faith of other Christians. But what are the differences which make Catholicism unique from other forms of Christianity? And why should a person be a Catholic rather than a Protestant? And, finally, how does a Catholic view his Christian brothers and sisters in different communities? These are the questions we must now place before us.

Just as Christians can state that all the great faiths of mankind capture the experience at the heart of the universe (the experience of love which we Christians find fully and perfectly articulated in the life and teachings of Jesus), so Catholic Christians today insist that all of the traditional Christian communities (the Orthodox churches, the Anglican communion, and the traditional Protestant bodies) capture the experience at the heart of Jesus' life and teaching.

The Catholic articulation

It will be easier to describe the various forms of Christianity if we make certain very broad distinctions and then describe how the Roman Catholic Church considers herself in relation to the Christians in each grouping. The first general grouping of Christians we can call Catholic. These would include Christians in the Roman Catholic Church, the various Eastern Orthodox churches and certain parts of the Anglican (Episcopalian) Church. Catholic Christians view Christianity on the whole as it has been presented in this book.

The principal disagreement between Roman Catholics and other Catholics lies on the level of unity. In our history various situations have arisen which led to splits between the various churches. Thus today only the Roman Catholic Church recognizes the pope as the official head of the Church. For Roman Catholics the pope is the symbol of our unity with one another and with all past Christians in the one body of Christ. The other Catholic communions differ from the Roman communion on this one point.

As we have seen, one important aspect of the Christian experience is the feeling of unity with God and with one's brothers and sisters in Christ. This unity within the Christian Church is a sign to the world of the true unity which exists between the universe and God—the unity toward which Jesus calls all people. If this unity is to be shown forth, if it is to be made manifest, if it is to appear as a sign, then a concrete symbol of that unity is needed. The symbol of that unity is communion with the pope, the successor of Peter. Thus while Roman Catholics feel that we share the same faith with all of our Catholic brothers and sisters, still we feel that only in the Roman Catholic communion can the fullness of unity in Christ be displayed to the world, that only in this Church can the fullness of communion and unity with the body of Christ be experienced. This unity we share is a sign to the nations, calling all people to realize in our world the unity that truly lies at the heart of existence.

The Protestant consensus

The second grouping of Christians can be defined under the name Protestant. These Christians include the Lutheran churches, the Presbyterians, the Methodists, the Calvinists, the Baptists and Congregationalists. These churches and certain of their offspring share with Catholic Christians the same Scriptures and, to a certain extent, the same doctrines, sacraments, ethics and institutions, but, depending upon the particular church, there are definite differences in these areas as well. For example, the Lutheran churches have preserved some of the same structure as the Catholic churches by retaining the office of minister and bishop, but they differ from Catholic bodies in that they officially recognize only two sacraments.

In general the Protestants have tended toward an emphasis upon Scripture and the Word at the expense of sacraments. Catholic Christians admire the reverence for the Word of God found among Protestants, and the Roman Church today is attempting to rectify her own overemphasis upon sacraments at the expense of Word through the translation of the liturgy into the vernacular and through the renewed emphasis upon Scripture among Catholics. To a Catholic, however, the Protestant expression of Christianity seems too restricted to what one can hear. Protestants strike Catholics as underdeveloped in their understanding of the sacraments. These special symbolic rituals extend the experience of Jesus to every part of human existence and communicate that experience not only through word but through gesture, drama and the visual arts.

Further, the disagreements about dogma, ethics and structure, from a Catholic viewpoint, weaken the experience of unity even more than the purely political disunity among Catholic Christians. A fundamental disagreement about certain central Christian doctrines or the structure of Christian life or the importance of the sacraments as communicators of Jesus' experience leads the Catholic Christian (Roman as well as the other branches) to regard Protestant Christianity as not quite complete or perhaps not as rich as it could be in the articulation of the experience of Jesus. Naturally the Protestant churches judge the Catholic communions from their own vantage point, but it would be best to let them speak for themselves.

While these differences between Protestants and Catholics are not incidental or insignificant, nevertheless in spirt of our disagreements we are learning today that our agreements are much more important and infinitely more significant. Most of the faith of Catholics we have explored is much better referred to as the faith of Christians. Catholics and Protestants share the same stories, many of the same doctrines, the two central sacraments, pretty much the same ethics, and in certain instances the same social structures. Above all we share the same experience of Jesus, and this experience is helping both groups today to overcome their differences so that someday a new Christian Church may evolve that better fulfills the vision of Saint Augustine: "In essentials unity, in accidentals diversity, in all things charity."

The experience of the sects

We shall refer to the final grouping of Christians as the sects. These include various groups that split off from the mainstream Protestant churches. In some cases it is even questionable whether they should still be labeled Christian communities because they differ so much from both the Catholic and Protestant churches. Some of these sects do not even regard Jesus as their central figure, although they historically come from Christian origins. The mainstream churches must judge each sect on its own beliefs and practices. To the extent that the sect harmonizes with the broad Christian understanding of Jesus and his life, they can be considered valid Christian communities.

However, in all the sects there are serious differences from traditional Christianity, to such an extent that some should be regarded as new religions or faiths. Roman Catholics make no judgment upon the validity of the experience shared in these different groups, but their articulation of the life and teachings of Jesus must be considered as deviating seriously from the main Christian tradition.

Thus if we believe that the purity of teaching about Jesus lies in the Catholic tradition, we should have to say that these groups no longer possess that teaching without serious distortion, and in some instances, such as Unitarianism, it is better to regard these people as of a different faith than Christianity. Again such a judgment implies nothing concerning the validity of their experience concerning life's meaning. We are only making a judgment of their articulation of that experience from a Christian vantage point.

Fare forward, but, above all, fare well

We have now completed our journey, and we have even paused for a while to explore from our vantage point the journey of other people to other cities. Each of our pilgrimages toward the source of meaning must remain to a great extent a very personal experience. However, as your guide I would like to share with you a few of my own observations here at our tour's end.

If, like me, you are a Roman Catholic, I hope that now our religion is not as confusing as it was in the past. The last ten years have seen momentous changes in our Church, such as have not been seen for over four hundred years. Those changes have been hard for all of us, but in spite of the changes it is by and large the same faith we knew before. The changes only serve to help us experience our faith to a fuller extent. Already our children are coming to a better understanding of Jesus and his experience of God than we had in our childhood, and these changes will enable us to join more closely with our Protestant brothers and sisters as we build a Church universal enough to contain the whole experience of Jesus.

If you have traveled this journey as a Protestant, I hope that you now see the great agreements we share in common. Today all the Christian churches stand at a great moment of their history. Four hundred years ago the Protestant reformers forced the Catholic Church to re-examine her faith and reform her practice. Today the Second Vatican Council is challenging Protestants to do the same thing. Four hundred years ago, unfortunately, the results of our reforms were division, disunity and misunderstanding. Today our common efforts at reform are leading us toward harmony, understanding, and unity. Let us together look forward to the day when a new Christian Church evolves which is truly expressive of all that is best in our two traditions.

If you are a believer in another faith, I hope that this book takes away some of the strangeness in Christian belief and practice. As pilgrims we travel the same road, and if our conceptions differ, hopefully our goals are the same. We Christians have much to learn from you and from your great traditions. From the Jewish tradition we are rediscovering the rich heritage of Jesus. Today many Christian families join in the celebration of Passover, and there are Christians today who are learning about the great spiritual disciplines of the East such as Yoga and Zen. In the future may our peoples share our insights and our experiences more.

Finally, if you are a seeker, I hope this man Jesus and his message will help you on your way. If the vision you have met here speaks to you, if it gives voice to your hopes and dreams, if it looks out on the world from a pleasant vista, if it challenges your sinfulness and inspires your desires, come and join your brothers and sisters in following Christ. If this community of weak human beings we call the Roman Catholic Church looks to you like home, if in spite of its sins and faults you want to call it your own, there's a place set at the table for you.

But whatever the case, let us never cease asking questions, for there is a response. In the darkness there is a light, by the wayside there is a hostel, and at the heart of the stars and galaxies, at the core of the neutron and the electron, behind the inscrutabilities of the human personality, amid the coldness and impersonality of technology, bureaucracy and politics, there stands a Father ready to welcome us home, each and every one.